D1056208

A Dictionary of Yiddish Slang & Idioms

A Dictionary of Yiddish Slang & Idioms

FRED KOGOS

A Citadel Press Book
Published by Carol Publishing Group

Contents

Introduction: Why Yiddish Slang and Idioms?

The success of our first effort to preserve Yiddish, called *Instant Yiddish,* was so great that it prompted the author to continue with his work. When Hitler killed 6,000,000 Yiddish-speaking Jews and when Israel proclaimed in 1948 that Hebrew was to be the official tongue of the nation, these actions spelled the death-kneel of Yiddish. This was the pity of it all! And this the author did not want to see, for since its beginnings in the 11th century, Yiddish has been the mother tongue, the "mameh-loshen," of millions of Jews throughout Europe who eventually carried it throughout the world as they migrated to the United States, Canada, Latin America, Africa, Australia, and elsewhere. Yiddish, rather than Hebrew, was and is the language of communication among Jews—in common life, in stories, jokes, books, newspapers, the theatre and truly the Esperanto of the Western World. And—through its colorfulness, its target-accurate phrases, idioms and sayings—it exudes an aroma and a texture of refreshing magic and laughter as well as sober thought that has been handed down through the ages from generation to generation and country to country. The author is obsessed with the thought that with the loss of Yiddish, the Jews lose not merely a language, but the Jewish people! Hebrew is spoken only by about 2,000,000 people in Israel and a few abroad, while Yiddish is still spoken by, and known to, over 10,000,000 throughout the world! Yiddish is creeping into the English language more startlingly than is apparent, with even Webster's Third International Dictionary containing over 500 Yiddish (and some Hebrew) words.

Because of the author's determination to perpetuate this picturesque language, he has spent several years studying, talking, learning, gathering and codifying words, phrases, greetings, colloquialisms, idioms, proverbs, etc., wading through the many dialects—God bless them and our people!—to unify and simplify them. Thus, for the first time since Roman letters began to be used in the English language, a *Dictionary of Yiddish Slang and Idioms,* which utilizes Roman letters instead of Hebrew characters, is presented for those in the English-speaking world who desire to learn and enjoy some Yiddish without the necessity of learning the Hebrew characters used in Yiddish. Consequently, anyone who reads English will be able to read and learn Yiddish phonetically and to explore the vast riches of Yiddish idioms, sayings, and colloquialisms found in this collection.

The author is a world traveler, having visited 70 countries and spoken Yiddish in most of them. He is not a writer by profession; he started this *Dictionary of Yiddish Slang and Idioms* as a hobby and it turned into an obsession and love. He claims no lexicographic background nor scholarly pretensions. His great hope is that this work will be a monument to an idea and a spirit, and that this "storehouse" of Yiddish words and phrases may help to perpetuate Yiddish and the enjoyment of it in everyday life. With *Instant Yiddish,* the author's first work, *Yiddish Slang and Idioms* will make you quite popular in these days when it is considered quite "in" to be bilingual and speak Yiddish, or at least know some appropriate and timely Yiddishisms—words, phrases or expressions.

If you grew up in a Yiddish-speaking home, you learned some of the language. If you grew up on the Lower East Side of New York, or in any other Jewish quarter in the United States, then you were handed an opportunity on a silver platter and you learned your Yiddish accidentally. But if you didn't get the chance and now want it, and you cannot afford the time to go to school but still want to get on the Yiddish bandwagon—then *Yiddish Slang and Idioms* is for you!

This work was written primarily for those who are unfamiliar with Yiddish and for those who once knew Yiddish but have forgotten it.

In transliterating the Yiddish words into English letters, we have simply written the Yiddish words phonetically as if they were English. So it will be quite easy for you to speak Yiddish instantly and make friends or influence sales, or put some variety into your conversation. Moreover, since Yiddish is so universal a language, this work will enable you to make yourself understood—and get along—anywhere in the world where Yiddish is spoken. And that means practically everywhere. *Enjoy!*

FACTS ABOUT YIDDISH

Yiddish is spoken by about 10,000,000 people throughout the world. It is widely used in Russia, Poland, Rumania, France, England and other European countries. In the United States and Canada, in Israel, South Africa and other African countries, in Latin America, in New Zealand and Australia and wherever else Eastern European Jews emigrated to, Yiddish survives as a spoken language—in the home, on the streets, in the theatre, in literature, newspapers and the entertainment field. There is at this moment a strong revival of Yiddish throughout the United States.

Yiddish, whose principal parent is Middle High German, is also related directly to English as well as to the Hebrew, Russian, and Polish languages, and enjoys borrowings from other languages and countries along the routes Jews have painfully travelled since the 11th century, when Yiddish was born.

There are four principal accents in Yiddish: Lithuanian, Ukrainian (Galicia), Polish, and Western (German). That's where you get Litvaks, Galitsyaners and other territorial nicknames for Jews. The essential difference between them lies in the pronunciation—whether broad, long or short. We have the same differences in accents in the United States: Southern, New England, Midwestern, New Yorkese—but we all understand each other. In this work we use the standard form, based simply on the usage of the majority. You'll be understood in any Yiddish-speaking environment.

YOU ALREADY KNOW LOTS OF YIDDISH

Since Yiddish is descended from Middle High German, which is related to the Saxon part of Anglo-Saxon, many of the short and common English words are more or less analogous to their Yiddish counterparts. Also, we have many cognate words whose roots both in English and Yiddish are alike or similar. Only their pronunciations makes it difficult to recognize them. But their presence will be of great help to you when you speak Yiddish, and humorously enough, if you mispronounce such cognate words, as you would in broken English, they will usually come out as perfect Yiddish. Here are a few: *vinter* (winter), *zinger* (singer), *zumer* (summer), *hant* (hand), *gut* (good), *epel* (apple), *broyt* (bread), *orem* (arm), *bahken* (bake), *bod* (bath), *bord* (beard), *beis* (bite), *bruder* (brother), *breng* (bring), *hoys* (house), *putter* (butter), *kalt* (cold), *kiel* (cool), *kozineh* (cousin), *tochter* (daughter), *zin* (son), *fahl* (fall) and very many others, including numbers.

In addition to the above, words which closely resemble English, about 500 other Yiddish words have become part of our everyday language in their original form and are even found in Webster's Third International Dictionary. Among them are:

gezuntheit (good health; also, bless you!), *kindergarten* (kindergarten), *shlemiel* (clumsy dope), *shlimazel* (unlucky person), *mazel* (luck), *shmo* (patsy), *kibbitz* (to meddle), *shikker* (drunkard), *shalom* (peace and hello), *tzimmes* (fruit compote, also, in slang, "big deal"), *Bar Mitzvah* (confirmation), *gefilteh fish* (stuffed fish), *halavah* (candy made of crushed sesame seeds and honey), *kosher* (proper Jewish food; also, OK!), *mitzvah* (commandment, good deed), *bris* (circumcision), *shabbes* (Sabbath), *meshugeh* (crazy), *mishmash* (a mess, confusion), *shlumpf* (sucker, patsy), *shnook* (a dolt) and many others.

ADVICE ON PRONUNCIATION

Vowels:	Diphthongs:	Consonants:
a as in f*a*ther	ai as in s*a*y or m*ai*n	dz as in soun*ds*
e as in b*e*d	ei as in b*y* or h*ei*ght	g as in *g*o
i as in l*i*t or b*ee*r	oi or oy as in b*o*y	ch as in lo*ch* (Scottish)
o as in h*o*t	or v*oi*ce	or Ba*ch* (German)
u as in p*u*t	When 2 other vowels	r soft with no trill
	are together,	ts as in pa*ts*
	pronounce them	tsh as in *ch*urch
	separately.	zh as in sei*z*ure

Also, a number of letters and words of prefixes are used interchangeably—Ahf and Oyf, Nit and Nisht, Oi and Oy, Oo and U, S and Z and Tsu and Tzu.

IMPORTANT NOTES ON PRONUNCIATION

Ahf and Oyf: There are a number of words, diphthongs and phonemes whose spellings represent the pronunciations of their locale—Russia, Poland, Germany, etc., so that sometimes the same word has two phonetic appearances; for example, "ahf" and "oyf." As the author heard them or himself used them, so he recorded them here. Although every effort was made for consistency within this work, the author felt compelled to retain these pronunciations which sounded so natural to the ear. The attuned ear will appreciate this, although the educated eye would prefer "oyf" to "ahf."

"H" after the vowel: In many cases the letter "h" has been added to a word after the vowel, as in "ahf," "bohmer," and so on. The purpose of this is simply to warn you to broaden the vowel and to tell you that it is short and shouldn't be pronounced as in English. If you pronounce "ahf," as in the English, "after," you're wrong! "Ahf" must rhyme with the "a" in "harvest."

"H" at the end of the word: The letter "h" has been added to many words that end in vowels to make sure that you pronounce that vowel as a separate syllable.

ABOUT ACCENT

In words of two syllables, the accent falls mostly on the first syllable. In words of three syllables or more the accent falls mostly on the second syllable. Often a word is lengthened by prefixes or suffixes. In that case, the original accent is retained.

I hope this is not too *ongepatshket* (confusing) for you!

HOW TO USE THIS BOOK

This work is easy to use. It is divided into two parts: Yiddish-English and English-Yiddish, and includes popular and familiar (at least to knowledgeable Yiddish-speaking Jews) as well as odd and peppery words, sayings, phrases, proverbs, colloquialisms, maxims, curses, maledictions, taboos, vulgarisms and obscenities. All are accompanied by the most applicable definitions and literal meanings so that you may understand more clearly the figures of speech, particularly in the idioms, slang, curses, and proverbs. Each word is in *transliterated* Yiddish phonetically recorded into the Roman alphabet, and all you have to do is pronounce as written, keeping the pronunciation guide in mind.

The choices included are based on the author's personal life, research and extensive reading. But more important, this book represents the help and suggestions of hundreds of the author's friends throughout the world, to whom he is happily indebted and gratefully appreciative.

This book will prepare you for everyday life experiences by giving you Yiddish expressions that are constantly used in conversation so that you will be able to understand and be understood. And this holds true not only for the United States but abroad as well.

Yiddish is becoming so universal these days that knowing a little of it will facilitate daily contacts with Jews in your travels at home and abroad, help you in emergencies, make friends for you and give you altogether a pleasant feeling and a fascinating adventure. "For gezunterhait" (bon voyage) and "shalom alaichem" (peace be unto you)—and above all, "mazel tov" (good luck to you)!

A Dictionary of Yiddish Slang & Idioms

YIDDISH-ENGLISH

A bisel A little

A biseleh A very little

A braireh hob ich? Do I have a choice?

A braiteh daieh hoben To do all the talking (Lit., To have the greatest say or authority)

A broch! Oh hell! Damn it! A curse!

A broch tsu dir! A curse on you!

A broch tsu mir! Woe is me! I have been cursed! (Lit., A curse to me!)

A brocheh A blessing

A choleryeh ahf dir! A plague on you!

A chazer bleibt a chazer! A pig remains a pig!

A chissoren, di kaleh iz tsu shain! Too bad that the bride is too pretty (Said of a novel or unjustified complaint)

A dank Thanks, thank you

A deigeh hob ich I don't give a hang. I don't care. I should worry.

A deigeh hob ich? Is it my worry?

A farshlepteh krenk A chronic ailment; particularly a lingering one

A feier zol im trefen He should burn up!

A gezunt ahf dein kop! Good health to you (Lit., Good health on your head)

A gezunt dir in pupik! Thanks for a small favor! (Lit., Good health to your belly button!)

A glick ahf dir! Good luck to you (Sometimes used sarcastically about minor good fortunes) Big thing!

A glick hot dir getrofen! Big deal! (Sarcastic; lit., A piece of luck happened to you!)

A klog iz mir! Woe is me!

A klog tzu meineh sonim! A curse on my enemies!

A lebedikeh velt Happy-go-lucky people (Lit., A lively world)

A leben ahf dir! You should live! (And be well—and have much more!)

A lek un a shmek A worker who does his job insufficiently gives this; you get this when a hostess serves peanut-size hors d'oeuvres—and too few of them; neither here nor there (Lit., A taste and a smell)

A lung un leber oyf der noz Stop talking yourself into illness! (Lit., Don't imagine a lung and a liver upon the nose)

A magaifeh zol dich trefen! A plague on you!

A makeh unter yenem's orem iz nit shver tzu trogen Another man's disease is not hard to endure (Lit., A boil under another's arm is not hard to bear)

A mentsh on glik is a toyter mensh An unlucky person is a dead person (Lit., A man without luck is a dead man)

A metsieh fun a ganef It's a steal (Lit., A bargain from a thief)

A nar filt nit! A fool feels nothing!

A nar veist men nit kain halbeh arbet You don't show a fool something half-finished

A nechtiker tog! Finished! Gone! Fait accompli! Impossible! Nonsense (Lit., A yesterday's day)

A nishtikeit! A nobody!

A sach tsu reden, vainik tsu herren A lot to tell, little to hear

A shaineh, raineh, kaporeh Serves him (her) right! (Lit., A nice, pure sacrificial fowl)

A shainem dank dir in pupik! Thanks for nothing (Lit., Many thanks in your belly button)

A shandeh un a charpeh A shame and a disgrace

A shtik naches A great joy (Lit., A piece or slice of pleasure)

A sof! A sof! Let's end it! End it!

A yor mit a mitvoch It will take a long, long time (till Doomsday) (Lit., A year and a Wednesday)

Abi gezunt!   As long as you're healthy!

Abi tsu zein mit dir   As long as I can be with you

Achrahyes   Responsible

Aderabeh-ve'aderabeh   By all means

Ahf meineh sonim gezogt!   It should happen to my enemies!

Ahf mir gezogt!   I wish it could be said about me!

Ahf mir gezogt gevorn!   It should happen to me!

Ahf tsi 'lehaches; (ahf tsu loches)   In spite of everything you do, it still comes out wrong

Ahf tsores   In trouble

Ahfen goniff brent dos hittel   A guilty conscience; A guilty person is always sensitive (Lit., On the head of a thief, burns his hat)

Ahntoisht   Disappointed

Ahntoishung   Disappointment

Ahzes ponim   Impudent fellow

Aidel   Cultured

Aidel gepatshkit   Finicky, super-critical

Aidim   Son-in-law

Ain klainikeit   Big deal (Derisive; lit., A small matter, A mere bagatelle)

Aiver butel   Getting senile; absent-minded; mixed up

Alaichem sholom   To you be peace (The answer or response to the customary salutation, sholom alaichem, Peace be unto you)

Alef-bais   Alphabet; the first two letters of the Jewish alphabet; the beginning; common knowledge; ABC's

Aleh meiles hot zi!   She has all the virtues!

Aleh shusters gaien borves   All shoemakers go barefoot

Alevei!   It should happen to me (to you)! Would that it comes true!

Alteh moid   Spinster, old maid

Alter bocher   Bachelor

Alter Kucker (taboo)   A lecherous old man; a played-out person, even if young; a person unwilling to participate

(abbreviated to A.K.)

Altvarg   Decrepit person or thing

Amho'orets   Ignoramus, boor, peasant (also spelled "amorets)

An ain unaintsikeh   A one and only, rarity

An alteh machashaifeh   An old witch

An alter bakahnter   An old acquaintance

An alter trombenick   An old wreck, an old bum

Antshuldik mir.   Excuse me.

Arbeh kanfess   Sleeveless religious undershirt

Arein   In, into; Come in!

Aribergechapt di mohs!   Overdressed woman

Aroysgevorfeneh gelt   Money thrown out; money wasted

Arumgeflickt!   Milked! Plucked!

Arumgevolgert   Wandered around; loafed

Arumloifer   Street urchin; person who runs around

Az a yor ahf mir.   I should have such good luck. (Lit., Such a year to me)

Az drei zogen meshugeh, darf der ferter zogen "Bim bom."   The majority rules. (Lit., If three people say or do something screwy, the fourth has to go along.)

Az es klingt, iz misstomeh chogeh.   When people talk about something, it is probably true. (Lit., when bells ring, it is usually a holiday.)

Az och un vai!   Tough luck! Too bad! Misfortune!

Azoy?   Really?

Azoy gait es!   That's how it goes! So it goes!

Azoy gich?   So soon?

Azoy iz es!   That's how it is!

Azoy ret men tsu a taten?   Is that how you talk to a father?

Azoy vert dos kichel tzekrochen!   That's how the cookie crumbles!

Azoy zogstu!   That's what you (pl.) say!

Ba'al gaiveh   Conceited

Baba stories, bubba meisses   Grandmother tales, fairy tales, inventions (See also bobbeh meisseh)

Badchan   Jester, merry maker or master of ceremonies at a wedding; at the end of the meal he announces the presents, lifting them up and praising the giver and the gift in a humorous manner

Bagel   Hard circular roll with a hole in the center (like a doughnut) and a glazed surface

Bagroben   To bury; buried

Baitsim (taboo)   Testicles; eggs (The proper word for eggs is aier)

Baizeh chei-eh   Vicious animal (usually refers to an inhumane person)

Balagoleh   Teamster, waggoner, coachman, driver; vulgar man, one without manners

Balebatish   Fine, responsible, honorable

Balebatisheh yiden   Respectable Jews, men of substance and good standing in the community

Balabatishkeit   Household, property, substance

Balebos   Owner, the big boss; an orderly person, householder, head of family

Balebosteh   Housewife, hostess, capable homemaker (complimentary)

Balmelocheh   Artisan, skilled worker, mechanic

Balnes   Miracle-worker

Bal shem   Term applied to a faith-healer, magic-worker, miracle performer

Bal Simcheh   One who celebrates a happy occasion

Bal Toyreh   Learned man, scholar

Bal tsedokeh   Benefactor, philanthropits

Barabantshik   Drummer in a band

Bareden yenem   To gossip

Baren (taboo)   Fornicate; bother, annoy

Bareh mich nit   Don't bother me. Don't screw me around!

Bareh nit (taboo)   Don't fornicate around; don't fool around; don't annoy; don't bother (someone)

Barimer   Braggart, show-off

Bar-mitzvah   Boy who, upon the completion of his thirteenth year, accepts the responsibility of fulfilling the religious law; also the celebration of this event, of becoming a man (Lit., Son of commandment)

Baroygis   Angry, petulant

Bas   Daughter (Hebrew)

Bas-mitzvah   Girl who has reached the age when she is required to fulfill certain mitzvos (commands, obligations); the coming of age; a woman

Bashert   Fated

Bashert zein   To be destined

Basherter   Beloved; the fated one, the destined one

Bas-malkeh   Princess (Lit., Daughter of a queen)

Batlen   Egghead (Talmudic)

Baveibter   Married man (veib means wife)

Beblech   Beans

Behaimeh   Animal, cow (when referring to human being, means dull-witted or a fool)

Bei mir poilst du   It's O.K. with me

Ben   Son (Hebrew); zun, Yiddish

Ben toyreh   Learned man, scholar (Lit., Son of the Torah)

Bentshen lecht   Recite benedictions over lit candles on Sabbath eve and holidays

Bentshing   Anglicization of Yiddish word bentshen, to say grace

Beryeh   Efficient, competent housewife

Bes medresh   Synagogue

Billik   Cheap, inexpensive

Billik vi borsht!   Cheap as beet soup! A real bargain! A real buy!

Bist ahf ain fus?   Are you in a hurry? (Lit., Are you

standing on one leg?)

Bist meshugeh?   Are you crazy?

Biteh   Please

Blaich vi di vant   Pale as a sheet (wall)

Blintses   Cheese or jellied pancakes rolled in dough and fried in fat (The French call it crêpe suzette)

Blondjen   To wander; be lost, as in the woods or on strange roads

Blozen fun zich   Puffed with haughty pride; shows off

Bobbeh meisseh   Grandmother story (Figuratively, a fairy tale, an unbelievable story, a tall story)

Bobkes   Small things, triflings, peanuts, nothing, worthless (Lit., Excreta of sheep, goats)

Bocher   Bachelor, unmarried man, young man

Bohmer   Bum (masc., Americanism)

Bohmerkeh   Bum (fem., Americanism)

Boitshick   Little boy; affectionate term for boy or man (Americanism)

Bordel   Brothel, whorehouse

Borsht   Beet or cabbage soup

Borsht circuit   Hotels in the Catskill Mountain, New York, with an almost entirely Jewish clientele, who are fond of borsht (beet and potato soup); term is used by entertainers

Boruchu (Hebrew)   Bless ye

Boruch hashem (Hebrew)   Bless God!

Borves   Barefoot

Botshvineh   Spinach soup

Boych vaitik   Stomach ache

Brahv   Brave

Braiter vi lainger   He's so happy! (Lit., Wider than longer, as with a big wide smile)

Brech a fus!   Break a leg!

Bris   Circumcision; the ceremony of circumcision

Bris Mieleh   Circumcision

Bristen   Breasts, teats

Broch   Fracture, break (Figuratively, a curse)
Broitgeber   Head of family
Bronfen   Whiskey
Brust   Breast
B'suleh   Virgin
B'suleh-shaft   Virginity
B'sulim   Hymen
Bubbee (booh-bee)   Friendly term for anybody you like
Bubeleh   Endearing term for anybody you like, young or
old
Bubkes   Beans; a mere bagatelle; (Slang, see Bobkes)
Bubu   Insignificant mistake
Bulvan   Man built like an ox; boorish, coarse, rude person
Burtchet   Growled

Cancer-shmancer, abi gezunt Cancer-shmancer, as long as you're healthy! (Americanism)

Chaleshen To faint

Challah Sabbath twists of white bread (Made in a variety of forms for the various holidays of the year)

Chaloshes Weakness, nausea, faintness, unconsciousness

Chamoyer du ainer! You blockhead! You dope! You donkey! You ass!

Chanifeh Over-praise

Chap a gang! Beat it! (Lit., Catch a way, catch a road)

Chap nit! Take it easy! Not so fast! (Lit., Don't grab)

Chas v'cholileh! God forbid! Not really at all!

Chaver (pl., Chavairim) Friend, Mr., comrade, colleague

Chaverteh Friend (fem.), Mrs. Miss, companion

Chazen Cantor

Chazenteh Wife of chazen

Chazzer Pig, a piggish person

Chazzerei Swill; pig's feed; anything bad, unpalatable, rotten

Chei Eighteen; life; word formed by the combination of Hebrew letters meaning eighteen and life

Chei(im) Life; (Le'cheiim (to life) is used as a toast equal to Here's to you, Skol, Down the hatch, etc. Chei-im is also a favorite name among Jews, becoming Hyman, later Henry, Herbert and other variations)

Chei kuck (taboo) Nothing, infinitesimal, worthless, unimportant (Lit., human dung)

Chevreh Company, society, associates

Chmalyeh! Bang, punch; Slam! Wallop!

Chochem Wise man; (slang) a wise guy

Chochem attick A wise guy

Chochmeh Wisdom, bright saying, witticism (often sarcastically)

Cholileh!   God forbid! Perish the thought!

Choleryeh   Cholera; a curse, plague

Choshever mentsh   Man of worth and dignity; elite person; respected person

Chosid   Rabid fan

Chossen   Bridegroom

Chossen-kalleh   Bride and groom; engaged couple

Chosser daieh   Feeble-minded

Choyzik machen   Make fun of, ridicule

Chropen   Snore

Chupeh   Bridal canopy (Its four poles signify the four corners of the world, and support a blue cloth, symbolic of the heavens); the marriage ceremony itself

Chutzpeh   Brazenness, gall, cheek

Chutzpenik   Impudent fellow

Cristiyah   Enema

Cristiyer   Enema

Danken Got! Thank God!

Davenen Pray

Davening mincheh Recite the afternoon or mincheh prayers, which consist of selections from psalms plus the Sh'moneh Esrei (Eighteen Benedictions) (Note English suffix "ing." The verb is davenen.)

Deigeh nisht! Don't worry!

Den Adverb used with questions to connote about (for example: "vo den?" for what else? "vi den" for how else?); then

Der oybershter in himmel God (Lit., The One above in heaven)

Derech erets Respect

Derniderriken Berate, to humble somebody

Dershtikt zolstu veren! You should choke on it!

Di emmeseh schoireh! The real article!

Dingen Bargain, hire, engage, lease, rent

Dos gefelt mir This pleases me

Dos gelt iz tserunen gevoren! My money went down the drain!

Dos hartz hot mir gezogt My heart told me. I predicted it.

Dos iz alts That's all

Dos iz geven a mechei-eh This was a pleasure!

Dos zelbeh Likewise.

Drai mir nit kain kop! Don't bother me! (Lit., Don't twist my head)

Drai zich! Keep moving!

Draikop Scatterbrain; one who tends to confuse you; one who connives and twists the facts to serve his own purpose (Lit., turn-head)

Drek (taboo) Human dung, feces, manure or excrement; inferior merchandise or work; insincere talk or excessive flattery

Drek ahf a shpendel (taboo)   As unimportant as dung on
   a piece of wood
Du fangst shoyn on?   Are you starting up again?
Dumkop   Dumbbell, dunce (Lit., Dumb head)
Dybbuk   Soul condemned to wander for a time in this
   world because of its sins. (To escape the perpetual tor-
   ments inflicted upon it by evil spirits, the dybbuk seeks
   refuge in the body of some pious man or woman over
   whom the demons have no power. The dybbuk is a
   Cabalistic conception)

Ech A groan, a disparaging exclamation

Efsher Maybe, could be

Ehe! Nothing of importance (exclamation)

Ei! Ei! Yiddish exclamation equivalent to the English "Oh!"

Ei, gut! Great! Just great!

Eilt zich! Get a move on! Hurry up! Rush!

Eingeshpahrt Stubborn

Eingetunken Dipped, dunked

Einhoreh Evil eye

Eizel Fool, dope

Ek velt End of the world

Ekeldiker parshoya Disgusting fellow

El, eleh Suffixes denoting diminutive or affection

Emes Truth; on the level, on the square

Er bolbet narishkeiten He talks nonsense

Er drait zich vi a fortz in rossel! (taboo) Is he bewildered! Is he in a fog! (Lit., he squirms like a fart in a foggy soup)

Er est vi noch a krenk. He eats as if he just recovered from a sickness.

Er farkocht a kasheh He makes a mess.

Er frest vi a ferd. He eats like a horse.

Er hot a farshtopten kop. He's thick headed.

Er hot a farshtopteh nonyeh. He has a cold. He has a stuffed nose.

Er hot a makeh. He has nothing at all (Lit., He has a boil or a minor hurt.)

Er hot kadoches. He has nothing. (Lit., Malaria fever (ague) is all that he gets!)

Er hot modneh drochim. He has odd ways.

Er hot nit kain daieh. He has no say (authority).

Er hot nit kain zorg. He hasn't got a worry.

Er iz a niderrechtiker kerl!   He's a low down good-for-nothing.

Er iz shoyn du, der nudnik!   The nuisance is here already!

Er kert iber di velt!   He turns the world upside down!

Er kricht in di hoyecheh fenster.   He aspires to high places (beyond his reach); a social climber (Lit., He creeps on high windows.)

Er kricht oyf di gleicheh vent.   Trouble-maker; a man who criticizes things that don't exist or that are uncriticizable (Lit., He climbs up straight walls.)

Er kricht vi a vantz.   He's slow as molasses. (Lit., He creeps like a bedbug.)

Er kukt vi a hun in a B'nai Odom.   He doesn't know what he's looking at.

Er macht a tel fun dem.   He ruins it.

Er macht mir a shvartzeh chasseneh!   He makes a lot of trouble for me! (Lit., He makes my wedding black.)

Er molt gemolen mel.   He repeats himself. He re-hashes things over and over again. (Lit., He grinds ground flour.)

Er redt in der velt arein!   He talks nonsense! (Lit., He talks into the world.)

Er redt zich ein a krenk!   He talks himself into a sickness!

Er zitst oyf shpilkes.   He's restless. (Lit., He sits on pins and needles.)

Er toyg ahf kapores.   He's worthless. (Lit., He's good only for a fowl sacrifice.)

Er zol einemen a mieseh meshuneh!   He should go to hell! (Lit., He should meet with a strange death.)

Er zol vaksen vi a tsibeleh, mit dem kop in drerd!   He should grow like an onion, with his head in the ground!

Eretz Yisroel.   Land of Israel.

Es brent mir ahfen hartz.   I have a heartburn.

Es cholemt zich mir . . .   I am dreaming that . . .

Es gait nit!   It doesn't work! It isn't running smoothly!

Es gefelt mir.   I like it. (Lit., It pleases me.)

Es hot zich oysgelohzen a boydem!   Nothing came of it!
(Lit., There's nothing up there but a small attic.)

Es iz a shandeh far di kinder!   It's a shame for the
children!

Es iz bloteh.   That's nothing. That's worthless.
It's nothing. (Lit., It is mud.)

Es iz mir eingefalen a plan.   A plan occurred to me.

Es iz nit geshtoigen un nit gefloigen!   It never happened!
It doesn't make sense! (Lit., It was never standing and
never flying.)

Es iz noch do   There still is

Es iz (tsu) shpet.   It is (too) late.

Es iz vert a zets in drerd!   It is as futile as stomping on
the earth! (Lit., It's [not even] worth a knock on the
earth.)

Es iz zaier teier (billik).   It is very expensive (cheap).

Es ken gemolt zein.   It is conceivable. It is imaginable.

Es kein zein.   It could be.

Es ligt im (ir) in zinnen.   It's on his (her) mind.

Es ligt im nit in zinnen.   He doesn't give a damn.
(Lit., It's not on his mind.)

Es macht mir nit oys.   It doesn't matter to me.

Es macht nit oys.   It makes no difference. It doesn't
matter. It isn't important.

Es past nit.   It is not becoming. It is not fitting.

Es past zich vi a patsh tsu gut shabbes!   It's bad manners.
It's not to the point. (Lit., It fits like a slap in the face
in response to the greeting: Good Sabbath.)

Es tut mir a groisseh hanoeh!   It gives me great pleasure!
(often said sarcaastically)

Es tut mir bahng.   I'm sorry. (Lit., It sorrows me)

Es tut mir laid.   I'm sorry.

Es tut mir vai.   It hurts me.

Es veist zich mir oys   It appears to me

Es vert mir finster in di oygen.   I am fainting!
(Lit., It's getting dark in my eyes.)

Es vet gornit helfen!   Nothing will help!

Es vet helfen vi a toiten bahnkes!   It won't help (any)!
(Lit., It will help like blood-cupping on a dead body.)

Es vet kleken.   This will do. It will suffice.

Es vet zich alles oyspressen.   It will all work out.

Es vet zich oys-hailen far der chasseneh.   It will heal in
time for the wedding. (Told even to a child when it gets
hurt. The implication is that marriage is a cure-all.)

Es zhumit mir in kop.   There's a buzzing in my head.

Ess gezunterhait!   Eat in good health!

Essen mitik   Dine

Essen teg   Yeshiva students would arrange to be fed by
various householders on a daily basis in different houses.
(Lit., Eat days)

Faigeleh Little bird. Also, a pervert, fairy, homosexual, fag

Fang shoyn on! You may start now! Come on, get going!

Fangst shoyn on? Are you beginning again? Are you starting something?

Farantvortlech Responsible

Fantazyor Man who builds castles in the air

Farbissener Embittered; bitter person

Farblondzhet Lost, bewildered, confused

Farblujet Bending your ear

Farbrenter Rabid fan, ardent participant

Fardart Dried

Fardeiget Distressed, worried, full of care, anxiety

Fardinen a mitzveh Earn a blessing or a merit(by doing a good deed)

Fardrai zich dem kop! Go drive yourself crazy!

Fardrai zich dein eigenem kop vestu mainen s'iz meiner! Go drive yourself crazy, then you'll know how I feel! (Lit., Turn your own head around, and you'll think it's mine)

Fardross Disappointment, sorrow

Farein Society

Farfel Noodle dough, grated or chopped into barley-sized grains

Farfolen Lost

Farfoylt Mildewed, rotten, decayed

Farfroyren Frozen

Fargenigen Pleasure

Farglust Have a yen for

Farkuckt (taboo) Dungy, shitty

Farmach dos moyl! Shut up! Quiet. (Lit., Shut your mouth.)

Farmatert Tired

Farmish nit di yoytzres!   Don't mix things up!
   (Lit., don't mix up the holiday prayers.)
Farmisht   Mixed up emotionally; befuddled
Farmutshet   Worn out, fatigued, exhausted
Farnem zich fun danen!   Beat it!
Farshlepteh krenk   Fruitless, endless matter
   (Lit., A sickness that hangs on)
Farshmeieter   Highly excitable person; always on the go
Farshnoshket   Loaded, drunk
Farshtaist?   You understand?
Farshtopt   Stuffed up, cluttered
Farshtunken   Smells bad, stinky
Farshvitst   Sweaty
Fartrasket   Decorated (beautified)
Far-tshadikt   Confused, bewildered, befuddled, as if by
   fumes, gas
Farzorger   Head of family
Feckuckteh (taboo)   Dungy, shitty
Feh!   Fooey!
Feinkochen   Omelet, scrambled eggs
Feinshmeker   Person with fine taste; elite, hi-falutin'
Ferd   Horse, (slang) a fool
Fet   Fat, obese
Filantrop   Philanthropist
Filen zich opgenart   Disappointed
Finf   A $5 bill; five; a fiver
Finferel $5 bill
Finster un glitshik   Miserable (Lit., Dark and slippery)
(A) Finsteren sof   Horrible ending (Lit., A dark ending)
(A) Finster yor!   A curse! (Lit., A dark year)
(A) Finsternish   Plague; a curse (Lit., Darkness, gloom)
Fisfinger   Toes
Flaishik, (Flaishidik)   Meat or meat ingredients (must not
Flaishik, (Flaishidik)   Meat or meat ingredients (must
   not be eaten at the same meal with dairy, milechik,
   foods)

Focha   Fan
Foigel   Smart guy
Foiler   Lazy man
Folg mich!   Obey me!
Folg mich a gang!   Quite a distance! Quite a job!
Why should I do it? It's hardly worth the trouble!
(Lit., Follow me on an errand.)
Folg mich a gang un gai in drerd!   Do me a favor and
drop dead!
Fonfen   Speak through the nose. Unclear. To double talk.
(Er) fonfet unter   He bluffs his way out
Fonfevateh   Talking through the nose
For gezunterhait!   Bon voyage! Travel in good health!
Forshpeiz   Appetizer
Fortz (taboo)   Fart, wind-passing, flatulence, eructation
Fortzen (taboo)   Pass or break wind, flatulate, eructate
Frageh   Question
Frailech   Happy
Frassk   Slap in the face
Freg mich becherim!   Ask me another! How should I
know? Who knows? (Lit., even if you excommunicate
me, I cannot give you the answer.)
Freilein   Miss, young lady
Freint   Friend, Mr.
Fremder   Stranger
Fressen   Eat like a pig, devour
Fresser   Big eater, gourmand
Fressing   Gourmandizing (By adding the English suffix
"ing" to the Yiddish word "fress," a new English word
in the vocabulary of American Jews has been created.)
Froy   Woman, Mrs.
Frum, (frimer)   Pious, religious, devout
Fun eier moyl in Got's oyeren!   God should hear you and
do as you say! (Lit., from your mouth to God's ears)
Funfeh   Speaker's fluff, error
Funfen   Speak through the nose; unclear; to double-talk

Gai avek!   Go away!

Gai bareh di vantsen!   Go bother the bedbugs!

Gai fardrai zich dein aigenem kop!   Go drive yourself crazy! Go mix yourself up, not me! (Lit., Go twist your own head.)

Gai feifen ahfen yam!   Go peddle your fish elsewhere! (Lit., Go whistle on the ocean)

Gai gezunterhait!   Bon voyage! Good-bye. (Lit., go in good health.)

Gai in drerd arein!   Go to hell! (Lit., Go down into the earthly grave.)

Gai kabenyeh mattereh!   Go to hell (Slavism)

Gai klap zich kop in vant!   It's useless (Lit., Go bang your head against the wall.)

Gai kucken ahfen yam! (taboo)   Don't bother me! Get lost! (Lit., Go defecate on the ocean.)

Gai plats!   Go split your guts!

Gai shlog zich mit Got arum!   Go fight City Hall! (Lit., Go fight with God.)

Gai shoyn, gai.   Scram! also, Don't be silly!

Gai strasheh di gens!   You don't frighten me! (Lit., Go threaten the geese)

Gai tren zich. (taboo)   Go frig yourself!

Gaien tsu kind   Going into labor to give birth.

Gait, gait!   Come now!

Gait es nit!   It doesn't work!

Galitsianer   Jewish native of Galicia

Gam atem   The same to you. (Hebrew)

Ganaiden   Garden of Eden; Paradise

Ganef   Crook, thief, burglar, swindler, racketeer

Gants gut   Quite well

Gantseh megilleh   Big deal! (derisive)

Gantser k'nacker!   Big shot!

Gantser mentsh Manly, a whole man, a complete man; an adult; a fellow who assumes airs

Gatkes Long winter underwear.

Gazlen Robber; criminal, racketeer, murderer

Geben shoychad To bribe

Gebentsht mit kinder Blessed with children

Gebrenteh tsores Utter misery

Gebrochener english Fractured English

Gechropet Snored

Gedainkst? Remember?

Gedarteh Dried

(Es) Gefelt mir I like it. It pleases me.

Geferlech Dangerous

Gifilteh fish Stuffed fish (Usually made of chopped fish, onions and seasoning, and cooked in salt water)

Gefilteh helsel Stuffed chicken-neck skin

Gefilteh kishkeh Stuffed derma (intestines)

Gehakteh english Fractured English

Gehakter hering Chopped herring

Gehakteh leber Chopped liver

Gehakteh tsores Utter misery (Lit., Chopped-up troubles.)

Geharget zolstu veren! Drop dead! (Lit., You should get killed.)

Gelaimter Person who drops whatever he touches

Gelibteh Beloved

Gelt Money

Gelt gait tzu gelt. Money goes to money.

Gembeh! Big mouth!

Gemitlich Slowly, unhurried, gently

Genaivisheh shtiklech Tricky, sharp, crooked actions or doings

Genug iz genug. Enough is enough!

Gesheft Business

Geshmak Tasty, delicious

Geshtank A stink, foul odor

Geshtroft Cursed, accursed; punished

Geshvollen Swollen, puffed up (Also applied to person with haughty pride)

Get Divorce

Gevaldikeh zach! A terrible thing! (often ironically)

Gevalt! See G'vald

(A) Gezunteh moid! Brunhilde, a big healthy dame

Gezunt vi a ferd Strong as a horse

Gezunterhait In good health

Gezunt-heit! Good health! (Use when someone sneezes or as a toast!)

Gib mir nit kain einoreh! Don't give me a canary! (Americanism, Lit., Don't give me an evil eye)

Gib zich a shockel. Get a move on.

Gib zich a traisel Get a move on

Gleichtseitik Likewise, simultaneously

Gleichvertel Wisecrack, pun, saying, proverb, bon mot, witticism

Gleichvort Proverb

Glezel tai Glass of tea

Glezeleh varems Tea (Lit., A glass of warmth)

Glick Luck, piece of luck

Gloib mir! Believe me!

Glusten tsu To have a yen for

G'nossen tsum emess! The sneeze confirmed the truth!

Goilem Dull person; clumsy and sluggish; mechanical man, robot

Goldeneh chasseneh Fiftieth wedding anniversary

Goldeneh medineh Golden country (meaning the United States)

Goniff Thief, same as ganef

Gornisht Nothing

Gornit Nothing

Got di neshomeh shuldik Innocent (Lit., All he owes is his soul to God)

Got hit op di naronim God watches out for or protects

the fools

Got in himmel!   God in heaven! (said in anguish, despair, fear or frustration)

Got tsu danken   Thank God

Got vaist   God knows

Got vet shtrofen   God will punish

Got zol ophiten!   God forbid!

Gotteniu!   Oh God! (anguished cry)

Goy   Gentile; non-observant Jew; a Jew unfamiliar with Judaism

Goyeh   Gentile woman

Goyisher kop   Used in Eastern Europe to imply slow-wittedness

Greps   Belch; a burp if it's a mild one

Gribbenes (grivvenes, greeven)   Small crisp pieces left from rendered poultry fat or skin, fried and eaten as a delicacy or combined with kasha groats or rice; cracklings

Grizhen mit di tsain   To grind one's teeth

Grizhidiker   Gnawing, grinding person

Grob   Coarse, crude, gross, profane, rough, rude

Grober   Coarse, uncouth, crude; blasphemous person

Grober finger   Thumb

(A) Grober yung   (See Gruber yung)

Grobyungish   Vulgar

Grois-halter   Show-off, conceited person

Grois vi a barg   As large as a mountain

Groisseh gedilleh!   Big deal! (said sarcastically)

Groisseh metsieh   Big bargain

Groisser fardiner!   Big breadwinner! (sarcastically said of person who isn't) (Lit., big earner)

Groisser gornisht   Big good-for-nothing

Groisser k'nacker!   Big shot! Big wheel!

Groisser potz! (taboo)   Big penis! Big prick! Big fool! Big shot! (Deragatory or sarcastic)

Groisser shisser   Big shot, big wheel

Gruber yung   Uncouth, rude, boorish young man
Gut far him!   Serves him right!
Gut Shabbes   Good Sabbath
Gut Yontev   Good Holiday
Guten tog   Good day; good-bye
Guts, (gits)   Good things—food, dollars, news, etc.
G'vald!   Cry of distress for help; wail of sorrow
   (Lit., Force, violence)
G'vir   Rich man

Hadassah Jewish women's organization which devotes iself to the maintenance of medical services in Israel (Hadassah means myrtle, a tree highly regarded by Israel of old; Haddassah became a favorite name for girls. Esther's name, as told in the Bible, was originally Hadassah. The women's organization bearing her name was founded on the Purim holiday of 1912)

Hagadah Book of services for the first two nights of Passover

Haimish ponem Friendly face, familiar face (from home)

Haiseh vanneh Hot bath

Haken a tsheinik Boring, long-winded and annoying conversation; talking for the sake of talking (Lit., To bang on the tea-kettle)

Hak flaish Chopped meat

Hak mir nit in kop! Stop bending my ear (Lit., Stop banging on my head)

Hak mir nit kain tsheinik Don't bother me (Lit., Don't bang on the tea-kettle)

Haldz-shvenkechts Gargle solution

Halevei! Would that it came true!

Hamotzi lechem min ho'orets Blessing over bread (Hebrew) (Lit., Who bringeth forth bread from the earth)

Hamoyn Common people

Handlen To bargain; to do business

Hartsvaitik Heart ache

Hartseniu! Sweetheart, my heart's love

Heizel Brothel

Hekdish Decrepit place, a slumhouse, poorhouse; a mess

Heldish Brave

Hert zich ein! Listen here!

Hetsken zich Shake and dance with joy

Hikevater Stammerer

Hinten   Rear, rear parts, backside, buttocks; in the rear
Hit zich!   Look out!
Hit zich vi fun a feier!   Watch yourself as if a fire
   threatened!
Hitsik   Hothead
Hitskop   Excitable person
Hob derech erets   Have respect
Hob nit kain deiges   Don't worry
Hoben chaishek tsu   To have a yen for
Hoben tsu zingen un tsu zogen   Have no end of trouble
   (Lit., To have to sing and to talk)
Hoizer gaier   Beggar
Hoi-echer drong   Long lean person
Hoizirer   Peddler (from house to house)
Holebshess   Stuffed cabbage
Holishkes   Stuffed cabbage
Holubtshes   Stuffed cabbage
Host du bei mir an avleh!   So I made a mistake. So what!
Hultei   Debauchee, person of loose morals
Hulyen   Raise Cain, to carouse

Ich bin ahntoisht   I am disapointed

Ich bin dich nit mekaneh   I don't envy you

Ich darf es ahf kapores   It's good for nothing! I have no use for it. (Lit., I need it for a [useless] fowl sacrifice)

Ich darf es vi a lung un leber ahfen noz   I need it like a wart on my nose (Lit., . . . like a lung and liver on my nose)

Ich darf es vi a loch in kop!   I need it like a hole in the head!

Ich eil zich (nit)   I am (not) in a hurry

Ich feif oif dir!   I despise you! Go to the devil! (Lit., I whistle on you!)

Ich fil zich opgenart   I am disappointed. (Lit., I feel cheated.)

Ich hob dir!   Go flap your ears! Drop dead! Scram! (Lit., I have you . . . !) (Americanism!)

Ich hob dich in bod!   I despise you! (Lit., I have you in the bath house!)

Ich hob dich in drerd!   I have you in hell! Go to hell! (Lit., I have you in the earth)

Ich hob es in drerd!   To hell with it!

Ich hob im feint   I hate him

Ich hob im in bod!   Forget him! The hell with him! (Lit., I have him in the bath house)

Ich hob im in toches (taboo)   "I have him in my buttocks." Usually said about someone you don't care for, or are angry with.

Ich vais.   I know.

Ich vais nit.   I don't know.

Ich vel dir geben kadoches!   I'll give you nothing! (Lit., I'll give you malaria or a fever.)

Ich yog zich nit.   I'm not in a hurry.

Ich zol azoy vissen fun tsores.   I should know as little about trouble (as I know about what you are asking me).

Iker   Substance; people of substance

Ikevater   Stammerer

In a noveneh   For a change; once in a blue moon

In di alteh guteh tseiten!   In the good old days!

In drerd mein gelt!   My money went down the drain!
(Lit., My money went to burial in the earth, to hell.)

In miten drinen   In the middle of; suddenly

Inten (hinten)   Behind, fanny, buttocks (slang)

Ipish   Bad odor, stink

Ir gefelt mir zaier.   You please me a great deal.

Iz brent mir ahfen hartz.   I have a heartburn.

Kaas (in kaas oyf)   Angry (with)

Kabaret forshtelung   Floorshow

Kabtzen, kaptsen   Pauper

Kabtzen in ziben poless   A very poor man (Lit., a pauper in seven edges)

Kaddish   Mourner's prayer, in praise of and submission to the will of God

Kaddishel   Baby son; endearing term for a boy or man (Derived from word "kaddish," which is a prayer for the dead that only males may recite)

Kadoches   Fever, malaria (Also means, ironically, less than nothing)

Kadoches mit koshereh fodem!   Absolutely nothing! (Lit., fever with kosher thread.)

Kaftan   Long coat worn by religious Jews

Kain ein horeh.   No evil eye! (Some say "don't give me a canary"; Lit., May no evil befall.)

Kakapitshi   Conglomeration

Kalamutneh   Dreary, gloomy, troubled

Kalleh moid   Girl of marriageable age

Kallehniu   Little bride

Kalyekeh   Cripple; misfit; also, anybody not good at their craft or sport

Kalyeh   Bad, wrong, spoiled

Kam derlebt   Narrowly achieved (Lit., hardly lived to see)

Kam* mit tsores!   Barely made it! (Lit., with some troubles)

*The word "Kam," also is pronounced "Kom" or "Koim" depending on the region people come from.

Kam vos er kricht   Barely able to creep; Mr. Slowpoke

Kam vos er lebt   He's hardly (barely) alive.

Kamtsoness   To be miserly
Kaneh   enema
Kaporeh, (kapores)   Atonement sacrifice; forgiveness; (slang) good for nothing
Karabelnick   Country peddler
Karger   Miser, tightwad
Kasheh   Groats, mush cereal, buckwheat, porridge; a mess, mix-up, confusion
Kasheh varnishkes   Cooked groats and broad noodles
Kashress   Kosher condition; Jewish religious dietary law
Kasnik, (keisenik)   Angry person; excitable person, hot head
Kasokeh   Cross-eyed
Katshkehdik (Americanism)   Ducky, swell, pleasant
Katzisher kop   Forgetful (Lit., Cat head)
Kazatskeh   Lively Russian dance
Kemfer   Fighter (usually for a cause)
Ken zein   Maybe, could be
(To) Kibbitz   To offer unsolicited advice as a spectator
Kibbitzer   Meddlesome spectator
Kiddish (Borai pri hagofen)   Blessing over wine or bread on the eve of the Sabbath or Festivals
Kimpet-tzettel   Childbirth amulet or charm (from the German "kind-bet-tzettel" meaning childbirth label containing Psalm 121, names of angels, patriarchs
Kimpetoren   Woman in labor or immediately after the delivery
Kind un kait   Young and old
Kinderlech   Diminutive, affectionate term for children
Kishef macher   Magic-worker
Kishkeh   Stuffed derma (Sausage shaped, stuffed with a mixture of flour, onions, salt, pepper and fat to keep it together, it is boiled, roasted and sliced)
(A) Kitsel   Tickle
Klainer gornisht   Little prig (Lit., A little nothing)
Klemt beim hartz   Clutches at my heartstrings

Klaperkeh Talkative woman
Klipeh Gabby woman, shrew, a female demon
Klogmuter Complainer, chronic complainer
(A) Klog iz mir! Woe is me!
Klop Bang, a real hard punch or wallop
Klotz Ungraceful, awkward, clumsy person; bungler
Klotz kasheh Foolish question; fruitless question
Kloymersht Not in reality, pretended (Lit., as if it were)
K'nacker Big shot; show-off; wise guy (Be sure to
  pronounce the first k)
K'naidel (pl., k'naidlech) Round dumplings usually
  made of matzoh meal and cooked in soup
K'nippel Button, knot; hymen, virginity; money tied in
  a knot in the corner of handkerchief
K'nish (taboo) Vagina
K'nishes Baker dumplings filled with potato, meat, liver
  or barley
Kochalain Summer boarding house with cooking
  privileges (Lit., cook by yourself)
Kochedik Petulant, excitable
Kochleffel One who stirs up trouble; gadabout,
  busy-body (Lit., a cooking ladle)
Kolboynik Rascally know-it-all
(A) Kop oif di plaitses! Good, common sense! (Lit., A
  head on the shoulders!)
Kopvaitik Headache
Kosher Food that meets rules of Jewish dietary laws;
  (slang) right, perfect, clean, proper
Kosher v'yosher! It's perfect! (Lit., It's legitimate.)
Kosokeh Cross-eyed
Koved Respect, honor, reverence, esteem
Krank Sick
Krank-heit Sickness
Krassavitseh Beauty, a doll, beautiful woman
Krechts Groan, moan
Krechtser Blues singer, a moaner

Krenk   Sickness, disease

Kreplach   Small pockets of dough filled with chopped meat or cheese which look like ravioli, or won ton soup, and are eaten in soup; (slang) nothing, valueless

Kroivim   Relatives

Kuck im on (taboo)   Defecate on him! The hell with him!

Kuck zich oys! (taboo)   Go take a shit for yourself!

Kucken (taboo)   To defecate

Kucker (taboo)   Defecator, shit-head

Kuckteppel (taboo)   Pot to defecate in

Kugel   Noodle or bread suet pudding, frequently cooked with raisins

Kuk im on!   Look at him!

Kum ich nit heint, kum ich morgen.   Mañana! Procrastinating (Lit., If I don't come today, I'll come tomorrow.)

Kumen tsu gast   To visit

Kuntzen   Tricks

Kuntzen macher   Magic worker, trickster

Kunyehlemel   Naive, clumsy, awkward person; nincompoop; Casper Milquetoast

Kurveh   Whore, prostitute

Kush in toches arein! (taboo)   Kiss my behind! (said to somebody who is annoying you)

Kush mich in toches! (taboo)   Kiss my behind! Stop annoying me.

Kushinyerkeh   Cheapskate; woman who comes to a store and asks for five cents' worth of vinegar in her own bottle

K'vatsh   Boneless person, one lacking character; a whiner, weakling

K'velen   Glow with pride and happiness, beam; be delighted

K'vetsh   Whine, complain; whiner, a complainer

K'vitsh   Shriek, scream, screech

Lachen mit yash-tsherkes Forced or false laugh; laugh with anguish

Laidik-gaier Idler, loafer

Laks See "lox"

Lamden Scholar, erudite person, learned man

Lang leben zolt ir! Long may you live!

Langeh dronitzeh Long lean girl (Lit., a long pole)

Langer drong Lean male

Lantsman (pl., lantsleit) Countryman, neighbor, fellow townsman from the old country

Lapeh Big hand

Lax Smoked salmon (see Lox)

(A) Lebedikeh velt! A lively world!

(A) Lebediker Lively person

(A) Leben ahf dein kop! Words of praise like: Well said! Well done! (Lit., A long life upon your head.)

Lebst a chazerishen tog! Living high off the hog!

L'chei-im, le'chayim! To life! (the traditional Jewish toast); To your health, Down the hatch, Skol

Leibtzudekel Sleeveless shirt (like bib) with fringes, worn by orthodox Jews

Leiden To suffer

Lemeshkeh Caspar Milquetoast bungler

Leveiyeh Funeral

Lig in drerd! Get lost! Drop dead! (Lit., Bury yourself!)

Ligner Liar

Litvak Lithuanian; Often used to connote shrewdness and also skepticism, because the Lithuanian Jews are inclined to doubt the magic powers of the Hasidic leaders; Also, a person who speaks with the Northeastern Yiddish accent.

Loch Hole; vagina (taboo)

Loch in kop Hole in the head

Loi alaichem! (Hebrew) It shouldn't happen to you! (Lit., May it not come upon you!)

Lokshen Noodles; also Italians, because they love spaghetti! (Americanism)

Loz mich tzu ru! Leave me alone! (Lit., Let me be in peace!)

Lox Smoked salmon (pronounced lahks)

Lishonoh tovoh tikosevu. (Hebrew) May you be inscribed for a good year (traditional greeting during the season of the High Holy Days).

Luftmentsh Person who has no business, trade, calling, nor income and is forced to live by improvisation, drawing his livelihood "from the air" as it were (Lit., air man); builds castles in the air; never achieves anything; a man who starves by his wits.

Mach es kailechdik up shpitzik. Come to the point!
(Lit., Make it round and pointy.)

Mach es shnel. Do it fast! Make it snappy! Hurry up!

Mach nit kain tsimmes fun dem! Don't make a big deal
out of it!

Machareikeh Gimmick, contraption

Machashaifeh Witch

Machen a g'vald Make an outcry; shout for help

Machen a leben Make a living

Machen a tel fun dir. Make a nothing out of you; ruin you

Macher Agent with access to the authorities who procures
favors for his clients for a fee, big shot; man with
contacts.

Macht zich nit visendik Pretends to be ignorant

(A) Magaifeh zol dich trefen! A plague on you!
(Lit., A plague should come to you!)

Mah nishtano? (Hebrew) What is the difference? (first
words in the opening "Four Questions" of the Passover
Hagadah, traditionally asked by the youngest child in
the household at the Passover Seder service)

Maidel Unmarried girl; teen-ager

Maideleh Little girl (affectionate term)

Maivin Expert, connoisseur, authority; sarcastically,
a know-it-all who really doesn't know it all

Makeh Plague, wound, boil, curse

Malech-hamovess Angel of death

Malech-hamovesteh Female angel of death; bad wife

Mamoshes Substance; people of substance

Mamzer Bastard (literally), disliked person, a trickster,
an untrustworthy person; a superlatively clever fellow

Manyeren Tact

Mashgiach Inspector, overseer or supervisor of Kashruth
(Jewish dietary observance) in restaurants and hotels

who makes sure everything is kosher

Matriach zein   Take pains; to take the trouble; to be so good as; please

Mazel tov!   Good luck. Loads of luck. Congratulations.

Mazuma, mezuma, mezumen   Money; ready cash

Me darf nit zein shain; me darf hoben chain.   You don't have to be pretty if you have charm.

Me hot alain ungekocht.   It's your own fault (Lit., You cooked it up yourself)

Me ken brechen!   You can vomit from this!

Me ken lecken di finger!   It's delicious! (Lit., [it is so good] one can lick his fingers!)

Me ken meshugeh veren!   You can go crazy!

Me ken nit puter veren!   You can't get rid of it (him, her)!

Me ken nit tantzen ahf tsvai chassenes mit ain mol.   Take it easy. Do one thing at a time. (Lit., you can't dance at two weddings at the same time!)

Me ken tzizetst veren!   You can burst!

Me ken zich baleken!   It's delicious

Me lacht mit yashtsherklis   False or forced laugh. (Lit., Laugh with lizard's laughter)

Me lost nit leben!   They don't let you live!

Me redt, me redt un me shushkit zich.   They talk and talk and say nothing.

Me redt zich oys dos hartz!   Talk your heart out!

Me zogt   They say; it is said.

Mechalel shabbes   Jew who works on or violates the Sabbath

Mecheieh   A great pleasure; something delicious, ultra delicious, life-giving, wonderful, superb, super-joy

Mechei-ehdik   Delicious tasting

Mechuten (pl., mechutonim)   Relatives through marriage, In-laws. Relationship of fathers of bride and groom.

Mechutonesteh   Mother of bride or groom—relationship to each other.

Megillah   Scroll or the Book of Esther; in slang, it means the whole works, the complete details, a long meaningless rigamarole.

Mehlech sobyetskis yoren Good old days (Lit., the years of King Sobyetski)

Meichel Delicacy, gourmet's delight; treat

Meileh Merit, asset, advantage, virtue

Mein bobbeh's ta'am! Bad taste! Old fashioned taste! (Lit., My grandmother's taste.)

Mein cheies gait oys! I'm dying for it! (Lit., my soul expires.)

Meineh sonim zolen azoy leben! My enemies should live so!

Mekler Go-between; broker, stockbroker

Meklerkeh Female broker, go-between

Melamed (pl., melamedim) Old style orthodox Hebrew teacher in "cheder"—one room school; a wise man

Melamedkeh Wife of a melamed

Men ken es in moil nit nemen Unpalatable (Lit., You can not put it in your mouth)

Menner vash tsimmer Men's room

Menorah Traditional Jewish seven-branched candlestick; also called menoyreh

Mentsh A special man or person. This word involves a whole philosophy of life. "Mentsh" means a human being in the moral and ethical sense; not merely a person, but a person with worth and dignity, one who can be respected.

Meshugass Crazy antics; craze; madness, insanity

Meshugeh Crazy

Meshugeh ahf toit! Crazy as a loon. Really crazy! Insane (Lit., dead crazy)

Meshugeneh Mad, crazy, insane woman; an eccentric female

Meshugeneh gens, meshugeneh gribbenes Goofy parents, goofy children (Lit., crazy fowl, bad cracklings or chitterlings)

(A) Meshugeneh velt!   A crazy world!

Meshugener   Mad, crazy, insane man; an eccentric male

Meshugener mamzer!   Crazy bastard!

Metsiyeh   Bargain, a find, a favorable purchase

Meyuches   Elite, cultured

Mezuma, mezumen   Money; ready cash

Mezuzah   Tiny box affixed to the right side of the doorway of Jewish homes containing a small portion of Deuteronomy (vi. 4-9 and xi 13-2') in twenty-two lines, handwritten on parchment.

Mich shrekt men nit!   You don't frighten me! They don't frighten me! It doesn't frighten me!

Mies   Ugly

Mies un mos   Tedious, abnoxious

Mieskeit   Ugly thing or person

Miesseh meshuneh   To wish lots of trouble on someone (Lit., a strange death or a tragic end)

Miesser nefesh   Cheap person

Mikveh   Indoor bath or pool required for Jewish **ritual purification,** particularly during and after menstruation; A bride-to-be always goes to the mikveh before the wedding.

Milchikeh   Jewish religious dietary laws distinguishes between two chief types of food: the milchikeh (dairy) and the flaishikeh (meat) which may not be eaten together; also, cutlery, dishes and utensils have to be kept separately

Milchiks   All dairy foods and cutlery, dishes and cooking utensils used exclusively for dairy foods according to Jewish ritual regulations. Also pronounced Milechiks. Comes from the word "milch"—milk.

Minyan   Quorum of ten men necessary for holding public worship (Young boys can also be included, provided they are over thirteen)

Mir bamien zich shtarker!   We try harder!

Mir velen bentshen.   We shall say grace.

Mir velen im bagroben!   We'll bury him!

Mir zolen zich bagegenen ahf simches.   May we meet on happy occasions.

Mirtsishem   (Hebrew) God willing (Contraction of Im Yirtseh Hashem)

Mirtsishem bei mir!   It should happen to me, God willing!

Mishebairach (Hebrew)   A blessing (Lit., He who blessed [beginning words of invoking a benediction])

Mishmash   Mixture, mess, confusion, hodge podge, jumble

Mishpocheh   Family, relatives

Mishpocheh-zachen   Family affairs

Mittelmessiker   Average man; person who is neither smart nor dumb; hoi polloi

Mitten derinnen   All at once, suddenly

Mitsveh   Commandment, mostly always used to mean a good deed, as helping the poor or visiting the sick; according to orthodox Jewish belief, there are 613 mitsves which Moses handed down; 365 of them were prohibitions and 248 were positive commands or mitsves.

Mizinikil   Last or youngest child in family

Mizrach   East; eastern; the eastern wall; front row in the synagogue, row of pews where the foremost members of the congregation sit

Mogen Dovid   David's shield, a Jewish emblem; Star of David

Mohel   The religious functionary who performs circumcisions

Moid   Unmarried girl; a buxom girl; an old maiden; spinster. (Usually you would say "Alteh moid"—old maid.)

Moil-shvenkechts   Mouthwash

Moisheh kapoyer   Mr. Upside-Down! A person who does everything wrong or in reverse

Molodyets   Clever fellow; jolly good fellow

Mordeven zich   To work hard

Mosser Squealer
Mumcheh Expert
Mutek Brave
Mutik heldish Brave
Mutshen zich To sweat out a job
Muttelmessig Meddlesome person, kibbitzer

Na! Here! (in giving) Take it. Here you are. There you have it

Naches Joy; Gratification, especially from children.

Nacht falt tsu. Night is falling; twilight

Nadan Dowry

Nadven (Hebrew) Philanthropist, benefactor

Nafkeh Prostitute

Nafkeh bay-is Whorehouse

Naidlechech Rare thing

Nar Fool

Nar ainer! You fool, you!

Narish Foolish

Narishkeit Foolishness

Nash Snack, sweet, treat (between meals)

Nasher A continual eater of delicacies; person with a sweet tooth; nibbler, especially between meals

Neb Contraction of nebbish

Nebach. It's a pity. May it not happen to you. Also a noun meaning an unlucky, pitiable person.
A ne'er-do-well.

Nebbish Nobody; pitiable person, simpleton, weakling; shy, drab, awkward person

Nebechel Nothing, a pitiful person; or playing role of being one

(A) Nechtiker tog! He's (it's) gone! Forget it! Nonsense! (Lit., a yesterday's day)

Nekaiveh Female; derogatively, connotes prostitute

Nem zich a vaneh! Go take a bath! Go jump in the lake!

Neshomeh Soul, spirit; divine element in man; also refers to a child

Neshomeleh Sweetheart, darling, sweet soul
(Lit., Little soul)

Nifter-shmifter, a leben macht er? What difference does it make as long as he makes a living? (Lit., nifter means deceased.)

Nishkosheh Not so bad, satisfactory. (This has nothing to do with the word "kosher," but comes from the Hebrew and means "hard, heavy," thus "not bad." The French equivalent—pas mal.

Nisht do gedacht! It shouldn't happen! God forbid! (Lit., May we be saved from it! [sad event])

Nishtgedeiget Don't worry; doesn't worry

Nisht gefonfit! Don't hedge. Don't fool around. Don't double-talk.

Nisht geshtoigen, nisht gefloigen. It's not true whatsoever. You're not making sense! (Lit., Didn't stand, didn't fly.)

Nisht getrofen! So I guessed wrong!

Nisht gut Not good, lousy

Nisht naitik Not necessary

Nishtgutnick No-good person

Nishtikeit! A nobody!

Nishtu gedacht! It shouldn't happen! God forbid! (Lit., May we be saved from it [re: a sad event])

Nit kain farshloffener A lively person

Nit ahin, nit aher Neither here nor there.

Nit gidacht! It shouldn't happen! (Same as nishtu gedacht)

Nit gidacht gevorn. It shouldn't come to pass.

Nit kosher Impure food. Also, slang, anything not good

Nit heint, nit morgen! Not today, not tomorrow!

Nit oif undz gedacht! It shouldn't happen to us!

Nit shatten tzum shiddech. It won't hurt (him or her) in making a (nuptial) match.

Nito There is not

Nito farvos! You're welcome! (Lit., nothing to be thankful for)

—Niu Suffix denoting endearment

Noc hneileh! Too late! (Lit., Arriving after the closing prayers of the Day of Atonement. The last prayer on "Yim Kippur" is called "Ne-ileh," after which God has sealed the fate of a human being.)

Noch nisht   Not yet

Nochshlepper   Hanger-on, unwanted follower

Nor Got vaist.   Only God knows.

Nu?   So? Well?

Nu, shoyn!   Move, already! Hurry up! Let's go! Aren't you finished? (this has infinite meanings. Lit., So, already)

Nudnik   Pesty nagger, nuisance, a bore, obnoxious person

Nudje   Annoying person, badgerer (Americanism)

Nudjen   Badger, annoy persistently

Ober yetzt?   So now? (Yetzt is also spelled itzt)
Obtshepen   Get rid of
Och!   Exclamation of surprise, dismay or disapproval
Och un vai!   Alas and alack; woe be to it!
Oder a klop, oder a fortz (taboo)   Either too much or not enough (Lit., either a wallop or a fart)
Ohmain   Amen
Oi!!   Yiddish exclamation to denote disgust, pain, astonishment or rapture
Oi, a shkandal, (oy, a skandal!)   Oh, what a scandal!
Oi, gevald!   Cry of anguish, suffering, frustration or for help
Oi, vai!   Dear me! Expression of dismay or hurt Vai means woe)
Oi vai iz mir!   Woe is me!
Oisgeshtrobelt!   Overdressed woman.
Oisgeshtrozelt   Decorated (beautified)
Oisgetzatzket!   Overdressed woman.
Ois-shteler   Braggart
Oiver botel   Absentminded; getting senile
Okuratner mentsh   Orderly person
Oleho Hasholem (Hebrew)   May she rest in peace
Olov Hasholem (Hebrew)   May he rest in peace. Peace unto him!
Olreitnik!   Nouveau riche! Parvenu! (Americanism.)
On langeh hakdomes!   Cut it short! (Lit., without long introductions.)
Ongeblozzen   Conceited; peevish, sulky, pouting
Ongeblozzener   Stuffed shirt. (Lit., Puffed up)
Ongematert   Tired out
Ongepatshket   Cluttered, disordered, scribbled, sloppy, littered, confusing, muddled; overly-done picture or work

Ongeshtopt   Very wealthy (Lit., Stuffed up or with)
Ongeshtopt mit gelt   Very wealthy; (Lit., stuffed with money)
Ongetrunken   Drunk
Ongetshepter   Bothersome hanger-on
Ongevarfen   Cluttered, disordered
Onshikenish   Hanger-on
Onshikenish   Pesty nagger
Onzaltsen   Giving you the business; bribe; soft-soap; sweet-talk (Lit., to salt)
Opgeflickt!   Done in! Suckered! Milked! (Lit., Plucked out like a chicken)
Opgehitener   Pious person
Opgekrochen   Shoddy
Opgekrocheneh schoireh   Shoddy merchandise
Opgelozen(er)   Careless dresser
Opgenart   Cheated, fooled
Opnarer   Trickster, shady operator
Opnarerei   Deception
Orehman   Poor man, without means
Oremkeit   Poverty
Oybershter   God (Lit., The One above)
Oybershter in himmel   God in heaven (Lit., The One above in heaven)
Oych a bashefenish   Also a V.I.P.! A big person! (said derogatorily, sarcastically, or in pity)
Oych mir a leben!   This too is a living! This you call living?
Oyfen himmel a yarid!   Much ado about nothing! Impossible! (Lit., In heaven there's a big fair!)
Oyfgekumener   Come upper, upstart
Oyfgekumener g'vir   Parvenu, nouveau riche
Oys shiddech.   The marriage is off!
Oysgedart   Skinny, emaciated
Oysgehorevet   Exhausted
Oysgematert   Tired out, worn out

Oysgemutshet   Worked to death, tired out
Oysgeputst   Dressed up, overdressed; overdecorated
Oysgetsert   Emaciated
Oysvurf   Outcast, bad person
Oyver butel   Senile, absent-minded, mixed up

Paigeren zol er!   He should drop dead!
Pamelech   Slow, slowly
Parech   Low-life, a bad man (Lit., having scabs on head)
Parechavatter   Low-life, bad man
Parnosseh   Livelihood
Parshiveh   Mean, cheap
Parshoin   He-man
Partatshnek   Inferior merchandise or work
Parveh   Neutral food, neither milchidik (dairy) nor
   flaishidik (meat)
Paskudnik, paskudnyak   Ugly, revolting, disgusting
   fellow; mean, evil person; nasty fellow; punk
Past nit.   It isn't proper.
Patsh   Slap, smack on the cheek
Patsher.   A person who carries on work or sport in a
   slipshod, unbusinesslike, half-assed manner.
Patshken   Mess around, to soldier on job, to work or play
   half-heartedly; futz around, doing things in a
   time-wasting manner without adequate results
Patshkies around   Anglicized characterization of one
   engaged in patshken
Patteren tseit   To lounge around; waste time
Pavolyeh   Slow, slowly
Peeric (taboo)   Vagina
Petseleh   Little penis (affectionately applied to infant boy)
Phooey! fooey, pfui   Designates disbelief, distaste,
   contempt
Pipek.   Navel, belly button, gizzard; same as "pupik"
Pirgeh (taboo)   Vagina
Pishechtz (taboo)   Urine
Pishen (taboo)   Urinate, piss
Pisher (taboo)   Male infant; a nobody; a little squirt.
   (Lit., a urinator)

Pisherkeh (taboo) Female infant (affectionate term); a
  nobody! (derogative term when applied to adult females;
  Lit., little urinator)

Pishteppel Pee pot

Pisk Slang, for mouth (moyl); insultingly, it means big
  mouth, loudmouth; a mouthpiece.

Pisk-Malocheh Big talker—little doer! (man who talks a
  good line but accomplishes nothing; Lit., work by
  mouth)

Pitshetsh Coquette, chronic complainer

Pitsel Wee, tiny

Pitsvinik Little nothing

Plagen Work hard, sweat out a job, suffer

Plagen zich To suffer

Plaplen Chatter

Plats! Burst! Bust your guts out! Split your guts!

Platsen To burst, bust

Plyotkenitzeh A gossip

Pooh! Exclamation of disdain

Potz (taboo) Penis (insulting when you call a man that)

Poyer Peasant, rustic, farmer, boor, dullard

Preplen To mutter, mumble

Prietzteh Princess; finicky girl; (having airs, giving airs;
  being snooty) prima donna!

Prost Coarse, common, vulgar

Prostaches Low class people

Prostak Ignorant boor, coarse person, vulgar man

Prosteh leit Simple people, common people; vulgar,
  ignorant, "low class" people

Proster mentsh Vulgar man, common man

Proster oilem Common people

Pupik Navel, belly button, gizzard, chicken stomach;
  (also a term of teasing endearment)

Pupiklech Dish of chicken gizzards

Pushkeh Poor box (In every traditional Jewish home,
  odd coins are put in this, particularly on Friday after-

noon, before the Sabbath begins; money is used for the support of philanthropic and educational institutions)

Pustunpasnik   Loafer, idler

Putskeh   Something decorative, from "putsen," to decorate.

Pyesseh   A play, drama

Rachmones   Compassions, mercy, pity

Rav   Rabbi, religious leader of the community

Reb   Mr., Rabbi; title given to a learned and respected man

Rebiniu   "Rabbi dear!" Term of endearment for a rabbi

Rebitsin   Literally, the rabbi's wife (often sarcastically applied to a woman who gives herself airs, or acts excessively pious); pompous woman

Rechielesnitseh   Dowdy, gossipy woman

Reden on a moss   To chatter without end

Redn tzu der vant   Talk in vain or to talk and receive no answer (Lit., talk to the wall for all the good it will do you)

Redt zich ein a krenk!   Imaginary sickness

Reich   Rich, wealthy

Reisen di hoit   Skin someone alive (Lit., to tear the skin)

Ribi-fish, gelt oyfen tish!   Don't ask for credit! Pay in cash in advance! Cash on the barrel-head! Money on the table!

Riboynoy-shel-oylom! (Hebrew)   God in heaven, Master of the Universe.

Richtiker chaifetz   The real article! The real McCoy!

Rirevdiker   A lively person

Rolleh   Acting a role in a play

Rosheh   Mean, evil person

(A) Ruach in dein taten's taten arein!   Go to the devil! (Lit., A devil [curse] should enter your father's father!)

Ruf mich k'nak-nissel!   I did wrong? So call me a nut!

Ruktish   Portable table

68

Saichel Common sense, good sense; tact, diplomacy

Sara . . . ! What a . . . ! What kind of a . . . !

S'art eich? What does it matter to you? Does it matter to you?

S'art mich vi di vant! I don't give a care!

Se brent nit! Don't get excited! (Lit., It's not on fire!)

Se hert zich a raiech! It stinks! It gives off a bad odor.

Se shtinkt! It stinks!

Se tsegait zich in moyl! Yummy-yummy! (It melts in your mouth!)

Se zol dir grihmen in boych! You should get a stomach cramp!

Sha! (gently said) Please keep quiet.
(shouted) Quiet! Shut up!

Shabbes goy Someone doing the dirty work for others (Lit., gentile doing work for a Jew on Sabbath)

Shadchen Matchmaker or marriage broker; (There is the professional type who derives his living from it, but many Jewish women used to engage in matchmaking without compensation only from religious motives)

Shaigetz Non-Jewish boy; wild Jewish boy

Shaigetz ainer! Berating term for irreligious Jewish boy, especially one who blatantly flouts Jewish law; fellow of great audacity

Shain vi di zibben velten Beautiful as the seven worlds

Shaineh literatur Belles lettres

Shaineh maidel Pretty girl

Shainer gelechter Hearty laugh (sarcastically, Some laughter!)

Shainkeit Beauty

Shaitel, (sheitel) Wig (at the wedding the ultra-orthodox bride has her hair cut off and she wears a shaitel ever after)

Shalach mohnes   Customary gifts exchanged on Purim, usually goodies

Shalom   Peace (a watchword and a greeting) Shalom Alaichem—peace unto you; hello; also, Good-bye, So long; also spelled sholom

Shammes   Sexton, beadle of the synagogue, also, the lighter taper used to light other candles on a menorah, a policeman (slang)

Shandhoiz   Brothel, whorehouse

Shat, shat! Hust!   Quiet! Don't get excited!

Shatnes   Proscription against wearing clothes that are mixed of wool and linen

Shema (Hebrew)   Hear Ye! (the first word in the confession of the Jewish faith: "Hear O Israe!: the Lord our God, the Lord is One!" It consists of the following passages: Deut. 6:4-9; 11:13-21 and Num. 15:37-41

Shemen zich in dein veiten haldz!   You ought to be ashamed of yourself (Lit., You should be ashamed down to the bottom of your throat)

Shemevdik   Bashful, shy

Shenereh laigt men in drerd.   Prettier ones they bury! (implying the girl is ugly)

Shepen naches   Enjoy; gather pleasure, draw pleasure, especially from children

Shidech (pl., shiduchim)   Match, marriage, betrothal·

Shihi-pihi   Mere nothings

Shik-yingel   Messenger

Shikker   Drunkard

Shikseh   Non-Jewish girl (also used to imply an impious or wild Jewish girl)

Shinden di hoit   Skin someone

Shiva   Mourning period of seven days observed by family and friends of deceased

Shkapeh.   A hag, a mare; worthless

Shkotz   Berating term for mischivous Jewish boy

Shlak   Apoplexy; a wretch, a miserable person; shoddy;

shoddy merchandise

Shlak joint   Store that sells cheap, inferior merchandise, second-hand or cut-rate goods, where bargaining over prices is important (Americanism)

Shlang   Snake, serpent; a troublesome wife; penis (taboo)

Shlanger (taboo)   Long or big penis

Shlatten shammes   Communal busybody, tale bearer; messenger

Shlecht   Bad

Shlecht veib   Shrew (Lit., a bad wife)

Shlemiel   Clumsy bungler, an inept person, butter-fingered; dopey person, fool, simpleton

Shlep   Drag, carry or haul, particularly unnecessary things, parcels or baggage; to go somewhere unwillingly or unwantedly

Shleppen   To drag, pull, carry, haul

Shlepper   Sponger, panhanddler, hanger-on; dowdy, gossipy woman; stupid person, dolt; a free-loader, one who expects something for nothing

Shlimazel   Luckless person. Unlucky person; incompetent person; one who has perpetual bad luck (Everything bad happens to him; it is said that the shlemiel spills the soup on the shlimazel!)

Shlog zich kop in vant.   Go break your own head! (Lit., bang your head against the wall)

Shlog zich mit Got arum!   Go fight City Hall! (Lit., Go fight with God.)

Shlogen   To beat up

Shlok   A curse; apoplexy

Shlosser   Mechanic

Shlub   A jerk; a foolish, stupid or unknowing person, same as shlump; second rate, inferior.

Shlump   Careless dresser, untidy person, foolish, dumb person; a jerk; as a verb, to idle or lounge around

Shlumper   Same as shlump

Shlumperdik   Unkempt, sloppy

Shlumpf   Sucker, patsy, fall guy, second rater

Shlumpy   Sweaty, unkempt

Shmaltz   Grease or fat; (slang) flattery; to sweet talk, overly praise; gooey (food)

Shmaltzy   Sentimental, corny

Shmatteh   Rag, anything worthless

Shmeis   Bang, wallop

Shmek   A smell

Shmek tabik   Nothing of value (Lit., a pinch of snuff)

Shmeer   The business; the whole works; to bribe, to coat like butter, to be excessively kind for selfish gain

Shmegegi   Buffoon, idiot, fool. See shmendrik

Shmeichel   To butter up

Shmeikel   To swindle, con, fast-talk.

Shmendrik   Fool; nincompoop; an inept or indifferent person (or one to whom you are indifferent); a dope, shlemiel, simpleton

Shmirt zich oys di shich!   You're welcome (in my home) (Lit., Wipe your shoes clean)

Shmo(e)   Naive person, easy to deceive; a goof (Americanism)

Shmock (taboo)   Self-made fool; obscene for penis; derisive term for a man

Shmohawk   Anglicized variant for "shmock" (penis)

Shmontses   Trifles, folly

Shmooz; (shmuess)   Chat, talk

Shmoozen, (shmuessen)   To discuss or converse idly or pleasantly

Shmulky!   A sad sack!

Shmuts   Dirt, slime

Shmutzik   Dirty, soiled

Shnapps   Whiskey, same as bronfen

Shnecken   Little fruit and nut coffee rolls

Shneider   Tailor; in gin rummy card game, to win game without opponent scoring

Shnell   Quick, quickly

Shnook A patsy, a dolt, a sucker, a sap, a meek person easy to impose on; Casper Milquetoast; easy-going, gullible

Shnorrer A beggar who makes pretensions to respectability; sponger, chisler, moocher; a parasite, but always with brass and resourcefulness in getting money from others as though it were his right

Shnur Daughter-in-law

Schochet A ritual slaughterer of animals and fowl

Sholem alaichem Hebrew-Yiddish salutation, Peace be to you (The person greeted responds in reverse, Aleichem sholem, To you be peace. Equivalent to hello. How are you? How do you do? Good-bye)

Shoymer Watchman; historically refers also to the armed Jewish watchman in the early agricultural settlements in the Holy Land

Shoymer mitzves Pious person

Shoyn ainmol a' metsei-eh! Really a bargain

Shoyn fargessen? You have already forgotten?

Shoyn genug! That's enough!

Shoyn opgetrent? (taboo) Have you finished the dirty work? (Lit., Have you finished fornicating?)

Shpilkes Pins and needles

Shpitsfinger Toes

Shpitz bekitzur! Cut it short!

Shpogel nei Brand-new

Shreklecheh zach A terrible thing

Shprichvort (pl., shprichverter) Proverb, saying

Shtain reich Very rich (Lit., Stone rich)

Shtark, shtarker Strong, brave

Shtark gehert Smelled bad (used only in reference to food; Lit., strongly heard)

Shtark vi a ferd Strong as a horse

(A) Shtarker Tough guy, a roughneck, a strong-arm character; a bully

(A) Shtarker charakter A strong character

Shav   Cold spinach soup, sorrel grass soup, sour leaves soup

Shtik   Piece, bit, lump; a special bit of acting

Shtik drek (taboo)   Piece of shit; shit-head

Shtik goy   Idiomatic expression for one inclined to heretical views, or to ignorance of Jewish religious values

Shtik holtz   Dumb like a piece of wood (Lit., Piece of wood)

Shtik naches   Grandchild, child, or relative who gives you pleasure or satisfaction; a great joy (Lit., A piece of pleasure)

Shtik nar   A big fool! Some fool!

Shtikel   Small bit or piece; a morsel

Shtiklech   Tricks; small pieces

Shtilinkerait   Quietly

Shtinken   To stink

Shtoltz   Pride; unreasonably and stubbornly proud, excessive self-esteem

Shtrudel   Sweet cake made of paper-thin dough rolled up with various fillings—usually fruit and nuts—and baked

(A) Shtunk   A guy who doesn't smell too good, also also applicable to a female; a stink (bad odor); a lousy human

Shtup   Push, shove; vulgarism for sexual intercourse (taboo)

Shtup es in toches! (taboo)   Shove (or stick) it up your rectum!

Shul   Colloquial Yiddish for synagogue; said to have stemmed from Germans who, seeing Jews studying in the synagogue, mistook the synagogue for a shul or school; according to another opinion, from the Latin term, a schola', used by Italian Jews as meaning community

Shule   School

Shush!   Quiet!

Shushkeh   A whisper; an aside
Shushken zich   To whisper, to gossip
Shutfim   Associates
Shvachkeit   Weakness
(A) Shvartz yor!   A black year!
Shvebeleh   Highly excitable person. (Lit., a match)
Shvegerin   Sister-in-law
Shveig!   Quiet! Stop talking!
Shvengern   Be pregnant
Shver   Father-in-law; heavy, hard, difficult
Shver tsu machen a leben   It's tough to make a living!
Shviger   Mother-in-law
Shvindel   Fraud, deception, swindle
Shvindeldik   Dizzy, unsteady
Shvindilt in di oygen   Blinding the eyes; feeling dizzy
Shvitser   "A big producer" (who doesn't produce);
   a braggart
Shvitz bod   Steam bath
Shvoger   Brother-in-law
Shvontz (taboo)   Man who behaves stupidly, ungallantly,
   obscenely, or idiotically (Lit., tail); penis
   (uncomplimentary)
Sidder   Jewish prayer book for weekdays and Saturday
Simcheh   Joy; also refers to a joyous occasion, such as a
   birth, bar-mitzvah, engagement, marriage, etc.
Sitzfleish   Patience that can endure sitting (Lit., sitting
   flesh)
S'iz mir gut!   It's great!
S'iz oys.   It's over. It's gone!
Skotsel kumt   A caustic greeting used principally in
   reference to women
S'macht nit oys.   It doesn't matter.
Smetteneh   Sour cream; Cream
Sof kol sof   Finally
S'teitsh!   Listen! Hold on! How is that? How is that
   possible? How come?

Strasheh mich nit!   Don't threaten me!
Szhlob   Moron
Szhlok   Nincompoop; ne'er-do-well

T.O.T. (See Toches ahfen tish)

Ta'am Taste, flavor; good taste

Tahkeh Really! Is that so? Certainly!

Tahkeh a metsieh Really a bargain! (usually said with sarcasm)

Taiglech Small pieces of baked dough or little cakes dipped in honey

Tallis Rectangular prayer-shawl to whose four corners fringes (tzitzis) are attached (used by male Jews during morning prayers)

Talis koten Religious fringed garment

Talmud The complete treasury of Jewish law interpreting the Torah (Five Books of Moses) into livable law

Talmud Torah The commandment to study the Law; an educational institution for orphans and poor children, supported by the community; in the United States, a Hebrew school for children

Tamavateh Naive, simple-minded, feeble-minded

Tandaitneh Inferior

Tararam Big noise, big deal

Tashlich Ceremony of the casting off of sins on the Jewish New Year (crumbs of bread symbolizing one's sins are cast away into a stream of water in the afternoon of the Jewish New Year, Rosh Hashoneh

Tateh, tatteh, tatteh, tatteleh, tatinka, tatteniu Father, papa, daddy, pop

Tateh-mameh, papa-mama Parents

Tateniu Father dear (The suffix 'niu" in Yiddish is added for endearing intimacy; also, God is addressed this way by the pious; Tateniu-Foter means God, our Father

Tateniu-Foter God, our Father

Tefillin (phylacteries) (Leather cubes containing scriptural texts inscribed on parchment; they are a sign of the covenant between God and Israel. They are worn by males over thirteen years old; see Bar-mitzvah)

Teier   Dear, costly, expensive

Tei-yerinkeh!   Sweetheart, dearest

Telerel fun himel   Something unattainable; the moon on a plate (Lit., A plate from heaven)

Temp   Dolt

Temper kop   Dullard

Tinif   Worthless! (Lit., excreta)

T'noim   Bethrothal, engagement

Toches   Buttocks, behind, fanny

Toches ahfen tish! (taboo)   Put up or shut up! Let's conclude this! Come clean, buddy! (Lit., Buttocks on the table!)

Toches-lecker (taboo)   Person who will do anything to gain favor; brown-noser, apple-polisher, ass-kisser (Lit., Buttock-licker)

Togshul   Day school

Tog-teglech   Day-to-day, daily

Toig ahf kapores!   Good for nothing! It's worth nothing!

Toit hungerik   Starved, dead hungry

Tokus, (tokis, tuckus) (taboo)   Posterior, rectum, buttocks, ass, behind (variant of "toches")

Toonked (tunked)   Dunked, dipped

Traif   Forbidden food, impure, contrary to the Jewish dietary laws, or not prepared according to regulations (applied also to forbidden literature and other non-kosher matters)

Traifener bain   Jew who does not abide by Jewish law (derisive, scornful expression; Lit., non-kosher bone)

Traifeneh bicher   Forbidden literature

Traifnyak   Despicable person; one who eats non-kosher food

Tranteh   Rag; (used sarcastically) decrepit, useless, worn out

Tren zich (taboo)   Frig you! Go fornicate yourself!

Trenen   To tear, rip, rape
Tripper   Gonorrhea
Trogedik   Pregnant
Trog gezunterhait!   Wear it in good health!
Trombenik   A bum, no-good person, ne'er-do-well; a faker
Tsaddik   Pious, righteous person
Tsap mir nit mein blut!   Don't bleed me!
Tsatskeh   Doll, plaything; something cute (like a girl);
   an overdressed woman; a sexually attractive girl
Tsatskeleh der mamehs!   Mother's favorite! Mother's pet!
Tsebrech a fus!   Break a leg!
Tsedokeh   Spirit of philanthropy; charity, benevolence
Tsedrait   Nutty, crazy, screwy
Tsedraiter kop   Bungler
Tsedrumshket   Confused
Tsedrumshki   Befuddled
Tsekocht   Excited
Tsemisht   Confused, befuddled, mixed-up
Tshatshki   Toy, doo-dad; pretty girl (see tsatskeh)
Tshav   Cold spinach soup, sorrel grass soup, sour leaves
   soup (usually pronounced "shav")
Tshepeh zich nit tsu mir!   Don't bother me!
   (Lit., Don't attach yourself to me!)
Tshepeh zich op fun mir!   Get away from me! Leave me
   alone!
Tshepen   To annoy, irk, plague, bother, attack
   unwantedly
Tsevishen-shtotisheh telefonistkeh   Long distance
   operator
Tsegait zich in moyl   It melts in the mouth, delicious,
   yummy-yummy
Tsemishnich   Confusion
Tsetrogen   Absent-minded
Tsevildeter   Wild person
Tsiklen zich   The cantor's ecstatic repetition of a musical
   phrase

Tsimmes   Sweet carrot compote; (slang) a major issue made out of a minor event; a fuss over nothing

Tsitskeh   Breast, teat, udder

Tsnueh   Chaste

Tsores   Troubles, misery

Tsu kumen oifen zinen   To come to mind

Tsu shand un tsu shpot   In disgrace and humiliation

Tsutsheppenish   Hanger-on; unwanted companion; pest; nuisance

Tsum glik, tsum shlimazel   For better, for worse

Tu mir a toiveh.   Do me a favor.

Tu mir nit kain toives.   Don't do me any favors.

Tu mir tsulib.   Do me a favor. Do it for my sake.

Tuckus   (See Toches)

Tumel   Confusion, noise, uproar

Tumler   A noise-maker (person); an agitator, boisterer, roisterer

Tush   Buttock (refers only to an infant's)

Tut mir hanoeh   It gives me pleasure (also used sarcastically)

Tut vai dos harts   Heartbroken

Tzatzkeh   Ornament, toy; a dingus, doo-dad; a living doll, a sexually attractive girl; an overdressed woman; a playgirl (same as "tsatskeh")

Tzitzis   Fringes attached to the four corners of the tallis; the prayer shawl

Tzufil!   Too much! Too dear! Too costly!

Tzu tei-er   Too costly

Tzures   Troubles (same as tsores)

Um-be-rufen Unqualified, uncalled for; God forbid;
  (A deprecation to ward off evil)
Um-be-shrien God forbid! It shouldn't happen!
  (A deprecation to ward off evil)
Umgeduldik Petulant
Ummeglich! Impossible!
Umglick A misfortune, tragedy; when it refers to a man,
  it means a born loser; an unlucky one
Umshteller Braggart
Umzist For nothing
Un langeh hakdomes! Cut it short! (Lit., Without a long
  introduction)
Unterkoifen To bribe
Untershmeichlen To butter up
Untervelt mentsh Racketeer
Utz To goad, to needle

Vai! Woe, pain; usually appears as "oi vai!"

Vai iz mir! Woe is me!

Vais ich vos Stuff and nonsense! So you say!
(Lit., Know from what)

Vaitik An ache

Valgeren zich Wander around aimlessly

Valgerer Homeless wanderer

Vaneh Bath, bathtub, tub

Vantz Bedbug; (slang) a nobody

Varenikehs Pastry made of rounds of noodle dough
filled with jelly, fruit, or meat, and fried

Varfen an oyg To watch out; to guard; to mind;
(Lit., To throw an eye at)

Varnishkes Kasha with noodles; stuffed potato cakes

Vart! Wait! Hold on!

Vash-tsimmer Bathroom, washroom

Vash-tsimmer far froyen Ladies' room

Vash-tsimmer far menner Men's room

Vechter Watchman

Veibernik Debauchee

Veibersheh shtik Female tricks

Veis vi kalech! Pale as a sheet!

Vek-zaiger Alarm clock

Vemen barestu? (taboo) Whom are you kidding? Whom
are you fooling? (Lit., Whom are you screwing?)

Vemen narstu? Whom are you fooling?

Ven ich ess, hob ich zai alleh in drerd When I eat, they
can all go to hell!

Ver derharget! Get killed! Drop dead! (Also "ver
geharget")

Ver dershtikt! Choke yourself!

Ver farblondjet! Get lost! Go away!

Ver vaist? Who knows?

Ver volt dos geglaibt?   Who would have believed it?

Veren a tel   To be ruined

Vi a barg   Large as a mountain

Vi der ruach zogt gut morgen   Where the devil says good morning! (has many meanings; usually appended to another phrase)

Vi gait dos gesheft?   How's business?

Vi gait es eich?   How goes it with you?

Vi gaits?   How goes it? How are things? How's tricks?

Vi haistu?   What's your name?

Vi ruft men . . . ?   What is the name of . . . ?

Vi ruft men eich?   What is your name?

Viazoy?   How come?

Vifil?   How much?

Vilder mentsh   A wild one; a wild person

Vilstu . . .   Do you want . . .

Voglen   To wander around aimlessly

Voiler yung!   Roughneck (sarcastic expression)

Vo den?   What else?

Vortshpiel   Pun, witticism

Vos art es (mich)?   What does it matter (to me)? What do I care?

Vos barist du? (taboo)   What are you screwing around for? What are you fooling around for?

Vos bei a nichteren oyfen lung, is bei a shikkeren oyfen tsung.   What a sober man has on his lung (mind), a drunk has on his tongue.

Vos draistu mir a kop?   What are you bothering me for? (Lit., Why are you twisting my head?)

Vos failt zai?   What are they lacking?

Vos gicher, alts besser   The faster, the better

Vos hakst du mir in kop?   What are you talking my head off for?

Vos hert zich?   What do you hear around? What's up?

Vos hert zich epes nei-es?   What's new?

Vos hob ich dos gedarft?   What did I need it for?

Vos-in-der-kort   Capable of doing anything bad (applied to bad person; Lit., everything in the cards)

Vos iz?   What's the matter?

Vos iz ahfen kop, iz ahfen tsung!   What's on his mind is on his tongue!

Vos iz der chil'lek?   What difference does it make?

Vos iz der tachlis?   What's the purpose? Where does it lead to?

Vos iz di chochmeh?   What is the trick?

Vos iz di untershteh shureh?   What's the point? What's the outcome? (Lit., What's on the bottom line?)

Vos iz mit dir?   What's wrong with you?

Vos kocht zich in teppel?   What's cooking?

Vos macht dos oys?   What difference does it make?

Vos macht es mir oys?   What difference does it make to me?

Vos macht ir?   How are you? (pl.); How do you do?

Vos machstu?   How are you? (sing.)

Vos maint es?   What does it mean?

Vos noch?   What else? What then?

Vos ret ir epes?   What are you talking about?

Vos tut zich?   What's going on? What's cooking?

Vos vet zein (Que sera?)   What will be?

Vos vet zein, vet zein!   What will be, will be!

Vos zogt ir?   What are you saying?

Vu tut dir vai?   Where does it hurt you?

Vuhin gaistu?   Where are you going?

Vund   Wound

Vursht   Bologna

Vyzoso   Idiot (named after youngest son of Haman, archenemy of Jews in Book of Esther); also, penis

Yachneh   A course, loud-mouthed woman; a gossip; a slattern

Yachsen   Man of distinguished lineage, highly connected person; privileged character

Yarmelkeh   Traditional Jewish skull cap, worn usually during prayers; worn at all times by observant Orthodox Jews, to indicate that someone (God) is above them; also worn by Catholic prelates

Yatebedam   A man who threatens; one who thinks he's a big shot; a blusterer

Yeder mentsh hot zeineh aigeneh meshugahss.   Every person has his own idiosyncrasies.

Yedies   News; cablegrams; announcements

Yefayfiyeh   Beauty; woman of great beauty

Yenems   Someone else's; the other's (the brand of cigarettes moochers smoke!)

Yeneh velt   The other world; the world to come

Yenteh   Gaggy, talkative woman; female blabbermouth

Yentzen (taboo)   To fornicate, to whore

Yentzer (taboo)   Fornicator, whoremaster

Yeshiveh   Jewish traditional higher school, talmudical academy

Yeshiveh bocher   Student of talmudic academy

Yeshuvnik   Farmer, rustic

Yichus   Pedigree, ancestry, family background, nobility

Yiddisher kop   Jewish head

Yingeh tsats-keh!   A young doll! A living doll!

Yisgadal, vyiskadash (Hebrew)   First two words of mourner's prayer honoring the dead

Yiskor   Prayer in commemoration of the dead (Lit., May God remember.)

Yold!   Dope, boor, chump, hick

Yontefdik   Festive, holiday-ish; sharp (referring to

clothes)

Yontiff   Any Jewish holiday (also spelled yomtov and yontev from the Hebrew—"yom tov"—a good day.)

Yortseit   Anniversary of the day of death of parents or other relatives; yearly remembrance of the dead

Yoysher   Justice, fairness, integrity

Yukel   Buffoon

(A) Yung mit bainer!   A powerhouse! Strongly built person (Lit., A boy with sturdy bones)

Yung un alt   Young and old

Yungatsh   Street-urchin, scamp, young rogue

Yungermantshik   A young, vigorous lad; a newlywed

Zaft Juice

Zaftik Pleasantly plump and pretty (woman); well-stacked; sensuous looking (Lit., juicy)

Zaftikeh moid! Sexually attractive girl

Zaideh Grandfather

Zaier gut O.K. (Lit., very good)

Zaier shain gezogt! Well said! (Lit., Very beautifully said!)

Zeh nor, zeh nor! Look here, look here!

Zei (t) gezunt Be well! Good-bye! Farewell

Zei mir frailich! Be happy!

Zei mir gezunt! Be well!

Zei mir matriach Be at pains to . . . Please; make an effort.

Zei nit a nar! Don't be a fool!

Zei nit kain goylem! Don't be a fool! Don't be a robot!

Zei nit kain vyzoso! Don't be a damn fool! Don't be an idiot! also, don't be a penis! (taboo)

Zeit azoy gut Please (Lit., Be so good)

Zeit ir doch ahfen ferd! You're all set! (Lit., You're on the horse!)

Zeit (mir) moychel Excuse me! Be so good as . . . Forgive me!

Zelig Blessed (used mostly among German Jews in recalling a beloved deceased—mama zelig)

Zeltenkeit Rare thing

Zetz Punch, bang! Pow! Also slang for a sexual experience (taboo)

Zhaleven To be sparing, miserly

Zhlob A jerk; foolish, stupid, uncouth

Zhulik Faker

Zhumerei Whirring noise

Zhumet Makes a whirring noise

Zi farmacht nit dos moyl She doesn't stop talking

(Lit., She doesn't close her mouth)

Zindik nit   Don't complain. Don't sin. Don't tempt the Gods.

Ziseh neshomeh   Sweet soul

Ziseh raidelech   Sweet talk

Ziskeit   Sweet thing, sweetness (Also endearing term for child)

Zitsen ahf shpilkes   Sitting on pins and needles; being fidgety

Zitsen shiveh   Sit in mourning (Shiveh means seven, the number of·days in the mourning period)

Zitsflaish   Patience (Lit., Sitting meat)

Zog a por verter!   Say a few words!

Zogen a ligen   Tell a lie.

Zogerkeh   Woman who leads the prayers in the women's section in the synagogue

Zoineh   Prostitute

Zol dich chapen beim boych.   You should get a stomach cramp!

Zol dir klappen in kop!   It should bang in your head (as it's annoying me!)

Zol er tsebrechen a fus!   May he break a leg! He should break a leg!

Zol es brennen!   The hell with it. (Lit. let it burn!)

Zol Got mir helfen!   May God help me!

Zol Got ophiten!   May God prevent!

Zol ich azoy vissen fun tsores!   I haven't got the faintest idea! (Lit., I should so know from trouble as I know about this!)

Zol vaksen tzibbelis fun pipek!   Onions should grow from your navel!

Zol zein!   Let it be! That's it!

Zol zein azoy!   O.K.! Let it be so!

Zol zein gezunt!   Be well! It (you, etc.) should be well!

Zol zein mit glik!   Good luck!

Zol zein shah!   Be quiet!

Zol zein shtil!   Silence! Be quiet! Let's have some quiet!

Zolstu azoy laiben!   You should live so!

Zolst geshvollen veren vi a barg!   You should swell up like a mountain!

Zolst leben un zein gezunt!   You should live and be well!

Zolst ligen in drerd!   Drop dead! (Lit., You should lie in the earth!)

Zolst nit vissen fun kain shlechts.   You shouldn't know from bad (evil).

Zolst es shtipin in toches! (taboo)   Shove it up your (anus) rectum!

Zorg zich nit!   Don't worry!

Zshlob   Slob

Zuninkeh!   Dear son! Darling son!

ENGLISH-YIDDISH

ABC's Alef-bais

A.K. Alter Kucker (taboo)

A bad person (capable of doing anything bad or evil!)
Vos-in-der-kort

A big, good-for-nothing A groisser gornisht

A big healthy dame A gezunteh moid

A blessing Mi shebairach (sarcastically means a curse)

A blessing on your head A leben ahf dein kop; a brocheh
ahf dein kop (used to mean "Well said!" "Well done!")

A curse on my enemies A klog tzu meineh sonim

A curse on you! A broch tsu dir! A choleryeh ahf dir!
A finster yor ahf dir!

A fool feels nothing A nar filt nit

A great joy A shtik naches

A Hebrew school Talmud Torah

A little A bisel

A little nothing Shmendrik, nishtikeit, gornit

A lot to tell, little to hear A sach tsu reden, vainik tsu
herren

A lucky thing happened to you! A glick hot dich
getrofen!

A one and only An ain un aintsikeh

A person who drops whatever he touches Gelaimter

A pig remains a pig A chazer bleibt a chazer

A plague! A magaifeh! A finsternish!

A plague on you! A choleryeh ahf dir!

A shame and disgrace A shandeh un a charpeh

A smell and a taste (what you get when a hostess serves
peanut-size hors d'oeuvres—and too few of them)
A lek un a shmek

A strong character A shtarker charakter

Absent-minded Tsetrogen; oiver botel

Absolutely nothing! Kadoches mit koshereh fodem!

Accursed Geshtroft
(An) Ache Vaitik
Acting bit Shtik
Advantage Meileh
Agent with access to the authorities who procures favors for his clients for a fee Macher
Agitator Tumler (at a resort)
Alarm clock Vek-zaiger
Alas and alack! Och un vai!
All at once Mitten derinnen
All shoemakers go barefoot. Aleh shusters gaien borves.
Alphabet Alef-bais (the first two letters of the Hebrew-Yiddish alphabet)
Also a V.I.P.! Oych a bashefenish!
Amen Ohmain
Ancestry Yichus
Anecdote Meiseleh
Angel of death (male) Malech-hamovess (sarcastically, bad husband)
   (female) Malech-hamovesteh (sarcastically, bad wife)
Angry (with) Kaas (in kaas oyf), baroygis
Angry person Kaasnick, kaasen, farbrenter
Animal (cow) Behaimeh (when referring to human being, means dull-witted)
Animal (wild) Chei-eh, vildeh chei-eh
Anniversary of the death of a person Yortseit
Announcements Yedies
(To) Annoy Tshepen zich, tsutshepen
Annoy persistently Nudjen, tshepen zich
Annoying person Nudje, nudnik
Another man's disease is not hard to endure. A makeh unter yenems orem iz nit shver tzu trogen.
Antique Tranteh (refers to rag; sarcastically, worn out or useless)
Any Jewish holiday Yontiff, also spelled yomtov and yontev

Anybody no good at their job   Kalyekeh
Anything bad to eat or own   Chazzerei
Anything worthless   Shmatteh (Lit., rag)
Anxious   Fardeiget
Apoplexy   Shlak
Appetizer   Forshpeiz
Apple-polisher   Toches-lecker (taboo)
Are you beginning again?   Fangst shoin on? Haibst shoin on?
Are you crazy?   Bistu meshugeh?
Are you in a hurry?   Bist ahf ain fus?
Are you starting up again?   Du fangst shoyn on?
Aren't you finished?   Nu, shoyn?
Artisan   Balmelocheh
As futile as stomping on the earth   Es iz vert a zets in drerd
As long as I can be with you   Abi tsu zein mit dir
As long as you're healthy   Abi gezunt
As unimportant as dung on a piece of wood   Drek ahf a shpendel (taboo)
(An) Aside   Shushkeh
Ask me another! (To show indifference or ignorance)
Ass   Chamoyer, ezel, eizel
   Freg mich becherim
Asset   Meileh
Ass-licker (taboo)   Toches-lecker
Ass-kisser (taboo)   Toches-lecker
Associates   Chevreh, chaverim, shutfim
Assuredly   Tahkeh
Astonishment (exclamation)   Oi!
Atonement   Kaporeh
Attractive girl   Tsatskeh
(An) Authority   Maivin
Average man   Mittelmessiker
Aw, hell!   A broch!
Awful!   Geferlech!
Awkward person   Klotz, kunyehlemmel; nebbish, nebach

Baby son   Kaddishel (endearing term)

Bachelor, unmarried man   Bocher, nit baveibter, alter bocher

Back-handed slap   Frassk

Backside   Hinten

Bad   Shlecht, kalyeh

Bad odor   Ippish

(A) Bad man   Parech, parechavatter, oisvurf

Bad person   Oisvurf, vos-in-der-kort

Bad taste   Main bobbeh's ta'am (Lit., My grandmother's taste)

(To) Badger   Nudjen

(A) Badgerer   Nudje, nudnik

(A mere) Bagatelle   Bubkes, bobkes; ain klainikeit!

Baked dumplings (filled with potato, meat, liver or barley)   K'nishes (pronounce the K!)

(A) Bang   Chmalyeh, klop, zetz, k'nack

Bang your head against the wall!   Klop zich kop in vant!

Barefoot   Borves

Barely able to creep   Kam vos er kricht

Barely alive!   Kam vos er lebt!

Barely made it!   Kam mit tsores!

Bargain   Metsieh

(To) Bargain   Dingen zich, handlen

Bashful   Shemevdik

Bastard   Mamzer

Bath   Vaneh, bod

Bath-ritual   Mikveh

Bat at pains to, (please)   Zeit zich matriach

Be happy!   Zeit frailich!

Be so good, (please)   Zeit azoy gut!

Be so good as   Zeit moychel; zeit zich matriach

Be quiet!   Zol zein shtil! Zol zein sha!

(To) Be ruined   Veren a tel
Be well!   Zei(t) gezunt
Beadle of the synagogue   Shammes
(To) Beam   Kvelen
(To) Beam with delight and pride   K'velen fun naches
Beans   Bubkes, beblech
Beast   Behaimeh; (sarcastically, fool)
Beat it!   Chap a gang! Farnem zich fun danen! Gai avek!
(To) Beat up   Shlogen
Beautiful as the seven worlds   Shain vi di zibben velten
Beautiful woman   Krassavitseh
(A) Beauty   Krassavitseh, shainkeit, yefayfiyeh
Bedbug   Vantz
Beet soup   Borsht
Befuddled   Farmisht, tsemisht, tsedrumshki, tsetumelt, fartshadikt
Beggar   Shnorrer, hoizer, gaier, betler
Behind (buttocks)   Toches, inten, hinten
Belch   Greps
Believe me!   Gloib mir!
Belles lettres   Shaineh literatur
Belly-button   Pipek, pupik
Beloved   Basherter (fated); gelibteh
Bending your ear   Farblujet
Benefactor   Bal-tsedokeh, nadven
Benevolence   Tsedokeh
(To) Berate   Derniderriken
Betrothal   T'no'im, shidech
Bewildered   Farmisht, tsemisht, tsetumelt, farblondjet
Big bargain   Groisseh metsieh
Big boss!   Balebos
Big breadwinner! (Sarcastically said of a person who isn't) Groisser fardiner! Parnosseh gebber!
Big deal!   Ain klainikeit! (derisive expression; a small matter); gantseh megillah, groisseh gedillah; tararam; (sarcastically, about someone else) A glich hot dich

getrofen!
Big eater Fresser
Big healthy damsel Gezinteh moid!
Big hand Lapeh
Big mouth (sarcastic) Pisk, gembeh
Big noise Tararam
Big prick! Groisser potz! (taboo)
Big producer! (who doesn't produce) Shvitser!
Big shot (who thinks he's a big shot) Yatebedam;
  groisser gornisht; groisser potz (derogatory and taboo)
Big shot (big wheel) K'nacker; gantser k'nacker;
  groisser shisser; macher
Big talker, little doer! Pisk-malocheh!
Big thing! A glick ahf dir! (sarcastically used for little
  good fortunes that occur)
Bit Shtik, shtikel
Bit of acting A shtik
Bitter person Farbissener
Blabbermouth (female) Yenteh
(A) Black year! A shvartz yor!
Blasphemous person Grober yung, grobyon, grubyon
Bless ye! Boruchu! (Hebrew)
Blessed Zelig
Blessed be God! Boruch hashem (Hebrew)
Blessed with children Gebentsht mit kinder
Blessing over bread Hamoitzeh. The full blessing is:
  Boruch ato adonoi elo-hainu melech oilom hamotzi
  lechem min ho'orets.
Blessing over wine Kiddish. The full blessing is: Boruch
  ato adonoi elo-hainu melech oilom borai pri hagofen.
Blinding the eyes! Shvindilt in di oygen!
Blockhead! (Ass!) Chamoyer, du ainer!
Blues singer Krechtser
Blundering Farblondjet
(A) Blusterer Yatebedam
Boarding house with cooking privileges Kochalain

Boil Makeh
Boisterer Tumler; shaigets, shkotz
Bologna Vursht
Bon mot Gleichvertel
Bon voyage For gezunterhait! Gai gezunterhait!
(The) Book of services for the first two nights of Passover
 Hagadah
Boor Yold, amo'orets, amorets, poyer
Boorish young man Gruber yung
Boorish or coarse person Bulvan
Bore Nudnik
Born loser Shlimazel; umglicklecher
Borsht circuit The Catskill mountains where there are so
 many Jewish hotels (see Yiddish-English section)
Boss Balhabos (pl., balalbatim); balebos
(To) Bother Tshepen, bareh
Bothersome hanger-on Ontshepenish, tsutshepenish
Boy (affectionate) Boitshik, boitshikel (**Americanism**);
 yingel
Boy (becoming a man) Bar-mitzvah
Braggart Barimer, shvitser, ois'shteler, umshteller
Brand-new Shpogel nei.
Brave Mutik heldish; brahv; shtark
Brazenness Chutzpeh
Break a leg! Brech a fus!
Break wind Fortz, fortzen (taboo)
Breast Tsitskeh (taboo), brist, brust
(To) Bribe (slang) Shmeer, unterkoifen, geben shoychad
Bridal canopy Chupeh
Bride Kalleh
Bride and groom Chossen-kalleh
Bridegroom Chossen
Bright saying Chochmeh
Broker Mekler (fem., meklerkeh)
Brothel Bordel, shandhoiz, heizel
Brother-in-law Shvoger

Brown-noser   Tocheslecker (taboo)
(A) Brunhilde   Gezunteh moid
Buckwheat   Kasheh
Buffoon   Shmegegi, yold, shmendrik, yukel
Bum   Trombenik
Bum (he)   Bohmer ((Americanism)
   (she)   Bohmerkeh (Americanism)
Bungler   Klotz, shlemiel, shlimazel, tsedaiter kop
Burst!   Plats!
Burglar   Ganef, goniff
Burp   Grepts
Burst with frustration   Platsen
(To) Bury   Bagroben
Business   Geshefts
(The) Business (as, giving you . . .)   Snmeeren, onzaltzen
Bust!   Plats!
Bust your guts out!   Plats!
(To) Bust   Platsen
(A) Busy-body   Kochleffel
Butter-fingered   Shlemiel
(To) Butter up   Untershmeichlen, shmeichel
Buttocks   Toches, hinten, inten; tush (only applied to
   infant)
Button   K'neppel, k'nop
Buxom girl   Moid; gezunteh moid; zaftikeh moid
By all means!   Aderabeh-ve'aderabeh

Cancer-shmancer, as long as you're healthy
Cancer-shmancer, abi gezunt
Candlestick (seven-branched)   Menorah, menoireh
Cantor   Chazen
Cantor's singing   Tsiklen zich
Capable housewife and homemaker (complimentary
term)   Balebosteh, beryeh
Careless dresser   Shlump, opgelozen(er)
Carrot compote   Tsimmes
(To) Carouse   Hulyen
(To) Carry   Shlepen
(To) Carry or pull an extra object or person   Shlep,
shlepen
Cash   Mezuma, mezumen
Cash only! Don't ask for credit!   Ribi-fish, gelt ah-fen tish!
Cash on the barrel-head!   Ribi-fish, gelt ah-fen tish!
Casper Milquetoast   Kunyehlemel, shnook, lemeshkeh
Casting off sins on the New Year   Tashlich
Caustic greeting (used in reference to women)   Skotsel
kumt!
Ceremony of the casting off of sins on the New Year
Tashlich
Certainly!   Tahkeh!
Charity   Tsdokeh
Chaste (applied to a female)   Frum, opgehit, tsnueh
Chat   Shmu'es
(To) Chat   Shmuessen
(To) Chatter   Plaplen
Chattering   Reden on a moss; Yatatata
Cheap (price)   Billik
(person)   Parshiveh, parech, mieser nefesh, karger
Cheap as soup   Billik vi borsht (a real bargain!)
Cheap skate (female)   Kushinyerkeh, mark-yiddeneh

Cheap skate (male)   Karger, mieser oisvorf
(To) Cheat   Yentzen, opnaren
(A) Cheater   Yentzer, shvindler, oisvorf
Cheated   Opgenart, opgeyentzt
Cheek (impudence)   Chutzpeh
Cheese or jellied pancakes rolled in dough and fried in fat
   Blintses
Chicken gizzards   Pupiklech
Child   Shtik naches (Lit., Piece of joy); kind
Child (youngest in family)   Mizinikil
Childbirth amulet (or charm)   Kimpet-tzettel
Children   Kinder
Children (affectionate term)   Kinderlech
Chiseler   Shnorrer
Choke yourself!   Ver dershtikt!
Cholera   Chalerya, choleryeh
Chopped herring   Gehakteh hering
Chopped liver   Gehakteh leber
Chopped meat   Hak flaish
Chronic ailment   Farshlepteh krenk
Chronic complainer   Pitshetsh, klogmuter (masc. and
   fem.)
Chump   Yold
Circumcision, (the ceremony of circumcision)   Bris, bris
   mieleh
Circumciser (man who performs ritual of circumcision)
   Mohel
Clever fellow   Molodyets
Clumsy bungler   Shlemiel, kunyeh-lemel, lemeshkeh,
   shlimazel
Clumsy, sluggish person (robot-type)   Golem, goilem
Clumsy person   Klotz, kunyehlemel, shlemiel, shmendrek,
   shlimazel, lemeshkeh
Clutched at my heartstrings   Klemt mir beim hartz
Cluttered   Ongepatschket, ongervarfen
Coachman   Balagoleh

Coarse Grob, prost

(A) Coarse person Grober yung, bulvan, grober, prostak, grubyan

Coarse, loud-mouthed woman Yachneh, yenteh

Coat like butter (bribe) Shmeer

Coat (long) worn by ultra religious Jews Kaftan

Coffee cake (like Danish pastry) Shnecken

Cold spinach soup Tshav

Colleague Chaver (pl., chavairim)

Come in! Arein! Kumt arein!

Come now! Gait, gait!

(To) Come to mind Tsu kumen oifen zinen

Come to the point! Mach es kalechdik un shpitzik! Nit gandjet!

Come-upper Oyfgekumener; olreitnik (Americanism)

Commandment Mitzveh, di (-s)

Commandment to study the Law Talmud torah

Commemoration service of the dead Yiskor

Common Prost

Common man Proster mentsh

Common people Prosteh leit, proster oilem, hamoyn

Common sense; good sense Saichel; mit a kop oif the plaitses

Communal busybody Shlatten-shammes

Company (of people) Chevreh

Compassion Rachmones

Competent housewife Balebosteh, beryeh

Complain K'vetsh, klogen

Complainer K'vetsher, klogmuter (male and fem.)

Complaint (of a novel sort) A chissoren, di kaleh is tsu shain

Complete details Gantseh megilleh (slang)

Compulsive eater Fresser

Comrade Chaver (pl., chavairim)

(To) Con Shmeikel

Conceited Ongeblozzen, grois-halter, ba'al gaiveh

Confused Tsemisht, tsetumelt, tsedrumshket
Confusing (work) Ongepatshket
Confusion (noise) Tumel, tsemishnich
Confusion (mix-up) (slang) Kasheh, mishmash
Conglomeration Kakapitshi
Congratulations! Mazel-tov!
Conniver Draikop
Connoisseur Maivin
Continuous eater of delicacies Nasher
Conversation Shmu'es
Cooked groats and broad noodles Kasheh varnishkes
Coquette Pitshetsheh, koketkeh
Corny Shmaltzy
Costly Teier
Could be! Ken zein! Efsher!
Countryman Lantsman, landsman (a fellow townsman from the old country)
Country peddler Karabelnick, hoizirer
Cow Behaimeh (sarcastically, dull-witted person)
Cracklings Gribbenes (or grivvenes, greeven)
Craze Meshugahss
Crazy Meshugeh, tsedrait
Crazy antics Meshugahss
Crazy as a loon! Meshugeh ahf toi't!
Crazy bastard! Meshugener mamzer!
Crazy man Meshugener
Crazy woman Meshugeneh
(A) Crazy world A meshugeneh velt!
Crepe suzettes Blintses
Criminal, murderer, racketeer (depending on your point of view) Gazlen untervelt mentsh
Cripple Kalyekeh
Critic who criticizes things that don't exist or that are uncriticizable Er kricht oyf di gleicheh vent!
Crook Ganef
Crooked actions Genaivisheh shtiklech

Cross-eyed   Kasokeh, kosokeh
Crude   Grob
Crude person   Grober yung, grobyan, grubyan
Cry for help   Oi g'vald! or just plain "G'vald!!!!"
Cry of anguish   Oi, g'vald!
Cry of distress for help (Lit., force, violence)   G'vald!!
Cry of suffering, or frustration   Oi, g'vald!
Curse   Choleryah, makeh, shlok; a broch! A finster yor!
   An umglik! A finsternish!
Cursed, accursed   Geshtroft
Curses!   A broch! A klog!
Customary gifts exchanged on Purim (usually goodies)
   Shalach mohnes
Cut it short!   Un langeh hakdomes! Shpitz bekitzur!
Cut-rate store   Shlak joint (Americanism)
Cute (like a girl)   Tsatskeh

Daddy Tateh, tatteh, tatteleh, tatinkeh, tatteniu
Daily Tog-teglech
Daily prayer book Sidder
Dairy dietary law Milchiks (milk product foods must not be eaten at same meal with meat (flaishik) foods); (adj.) Milchikeh or milichdik
Dairy foods Milchiks (of milk base content); milechiks
Damn it! A broch!
Danger Sakoneh
Dangerous Geferlech, sakoneh
Darling Neshomeleh, teiers
Darling son Zuninkeh
Daughter Bas (Hebrew); tochter (Yiddish)
Daughter-in-law Shnur
David's shield Mogen David
Day-to-day Tog-teglech
Dead hungry Toit hungerik
Dear Teier
Dear me! Oi vai!
Dear son Zunin-keh
Debauchee Hultei, veibernik
Decayed Forfoilt, tsefoilt
Deception Shvindel, opnarerei
Decorated (beautified) Oysgeputst, fartrasket, oisgeshtrozelt
Decorative (something) Putskeh
Decrepit person or thing Tranteh, altvarg, noiteh lomus
Deep sorrow or hurt Fardross
(To) Defecate Kucken (taboo)
Defecate on him! Kuck im on (taboo)
Defecator Kucker (taboo)
Delicacy Meichel
Delicious Tsegait zich in moyl

Delicious tasting   Geshmak, mecheieh, mecheiehdik
Delight   Naches, hanoeh, fraid, fargenigen
(To be) Delighted   K'velen
(To be) Destined   Bashert zein
Devout   Frum (frimer)
Dietary laws   Kashress
Diminutive suffixes   El, eleh
Diminutive, affectionate term for children   Kinderlech
(To) Dine   Essen mitek
Dingus   Tsatskeh
Diplomacy   Saichel, diplomatyeh
Dipped   Toonked, tunked, eingetunken
Dirt   Shmuts
Dirty   Shmutsik
Disappointment   Ahntoisht, zich filen opgenart
Disappointment   Ahntoishung, fardross
Disbelief, distaste, contempt   Phooey! Fuie! Fu zol es veren!
Disdain (exclamation)   Pooh!
(In) Disgrace and humiliation.   Tsu shand un tsu shpot
Disgust (exclamation)   Oi! (Please say this in a disgusting way—with a grunt-like sound coming deep from the throat!)
Disgusting fellow   Paskudnik, paskudnyak, ekeldiker parshoyn
Dismay   Oi vai!
Disordered   Ongepatshket, ongevarfen
Distressed   Fardeiget
Divorce   Get
Dizzy   Shvindeldik
(Feeling) Dizzy   Shvindilt in di oygen
(To) Do all the talking   A braiteh daieh hoben
Do it fast!   Maches shnel!
Do it for my sake.   Tu mir tsulib.
Do me a favor.   Tu mir a toiveh. Tu mir tsulib.
Do me a favor and drop dead!   Folg mich a gang un gai

in dr'erd!

(To) Do things in time-wasting manner   Patshken

Do you want?   Vilstu?

Does it matter to you?   S'art eich?

Doesn't worry.   Nishgedeiget

Doll   Tsatskeh, krassavitseh, yefayfiyeh

Dolt   Shnook, shlepper, temp

Done in!   Opgeflickt

Donkey, you!   Chamoyer du ainer!

Don't annoy me!   Bareh mich nit!

Don't ask for credit!   Ribi-fish, gelt ahfen tish!

Don't be a damn fool!   Zei nit kain vyzosoh!

Don't be a fool!   Zei nit a nar! Zei nit kain goylem!

Don't be an idiot!   Zei nit kain vyzosoh!

Don't be silly!   Gai shoyn, gai! Zei nit kain nar!

Don't bleed me!   Tsap mir nit dos blut!

Don't bother me!   Drai mir nit kain kop! Hak mir nit kain tsheinik! Tshpeh zich nit tsu mir! Tshepeh zich op fun mir!

Don't bother me!   Gai kucken ahfen yam! (taboo) (Lit., go defecate on the ocean!)

Don't complain.   Zindik nit. Baklog zich nit.

Don't do me any favors.   Tu mir nit kain toives.

Don't double talk.   Nisht gefonfet. Fonfeh nit.

Don't fool around.   Nisht gefonfet; bareh nit! (taboo)

Don't fornicate around.   Bareh nit! (taboo)

Don't get excited!   Shat, shat. Se brent nit!

Don't give me a canary; (don't give me an evil eye).   Gib mir nit kain einhoreh

Don't hedge.   Nisht gefonfet.

Don't make a big deal out of it!   Mach nit kain tsimmes fun dem!

Don't mix things up!   Farmisht nit di yoytzres!

Don't screw me around.   Bareh mich nit.

Don't sin!   Zindik nit!

Don't tempt fate.   Zindink nit

Don't threaten me! Strasheh mich nit!
Don't twist my head! Drai mir nit kain kop!
Don't worry! Deigeh nisht! Hob nit kain deiges!
  Nishtgedeiget! Zorg zich nit!
Dope Shmendrik, yold, chamoyer, eizel, nar
Dopey, clumsy person Shlemiel
Doo-dad Tshatshki, tsatskeh
(To) Double-talk. Funfen, fonfen
Dowdy, gossipy woman Shlepperkeh, rechielesnitseh
Down the hatch! Le'chayim, l'chei-im
Dowry Nadan
Drab Nebbish, nebach
(To) Drag, carry or haul (particularly unnecessary things
  or parcels) Shlepen
Dreary Kalamutneh
Dressed up (to the hilt!) Oysgeputst
Dried Gedarteh, dareh
Driver Balagoleh
Drop dead! Geharget zolstu veren! Ver derharget! Ver
  geharget! Zolst ligen in drerd! Lig in drerd! Ich hob
  dich! (mildest)
Drummer in a band Barabantshik
Drunk Shikker
Drunkard Shikker
Drunken, inebriated Shikker, farshnoshket
Ducky (swell, pleasant) Katshkedik
Dull person, clumsy and sluggish Goilem
Dull-witted Behaimeh, poyer
Dullard Temper kop, poyer
Dumb like a piece of wood! Shtik holtz!
Dumbbell! Dumkop!
Dumplings (round and cooked) K'naidlech
    (flat, filled and baked) K'nishes
Dunce Dumkop
Dung Drek (taboo)
Dungy Farkakteh, fekuckteh
Dunked Tunked, toonked, eingetunken

(To) Earn a blessing (by doing a good deed)   Fardinen a mitzveh

East   Mizrach

Eastern   Mizrach

Eastern wall in synagogue   Mizrach vant

Eat in good health!   Ess gezunterhait!

(To) Eat like a pig!   Fressen vi a chazzer!

Eccentric (man)   Meshuggener, tsedreiter
     (woman)   Meshuggeneh, tsedreiteh

Egghead (Talmudic)   Batlen

Eggs   Baitsim (taboo), aier

Either too much or not enough.   Oder a klop, oder a fortz (taboo)

Elite   Feinshmeker, meyuches, choshever mentsh

Emaciated   Oysgedart, oysgetsert

Embittered   Farbissener

End of the world!   Ek velt!

Endearing suffix   -Niu; el, eleh

Endearing term (for anybody you like, young or old)   Bubeleh, bubbee, tsatskeleh

Enema   Kaneh, cristiyer, cristiyah

(To) Engage (hire)   Dingen

Engaged couple   Chossen-kalleh

Enjoy   Shepen naches

Enough is enough!   Genug is genug!

Erudite person   Lamden

Esteem   Koved, derech erets

Every person has his own idiosyncrasies.   Yeder mentsh hot zeineh aigener meshugahssen.

Evil eye   Einhoreh

Excited   Tsekocht

Excitable person   Kasnik, keisnik, hitskop, farbrenter

Exclamation of disgust, pain, astonishmen or rapture   Oi!!

Exclamation of surprise, dismay or disapproval Och! Oh!
Exclamation of disdain Pooh!
Excrement (human) Drek (taboo)
Excuse me. Zeit (mir) moychel. Antshuldik mir.
Exhausted Oysgehorevet, farmutshet.
Expensive Teier
Expert Maivin, mumcheh
Expression of dismay Oy, vai! (vai means pain)
Expressman Balagoleh
Extreme pleasure Grois fargenigen

Fag Faigeleh (taboo)
(To) Faint Chaleshen
Fainted Gechahlesht
Faintness Chaloshes
Fairness Yoysher
Fairy tale Bobbeh meisseh
Fait accompli! A nechtiker tog! Farfallen!
Faith-healer Bal Shem
Faker Trombenik, zhulyik
Fall guy Shlumpf; seir l'azozel (Hebrew for scapegoat)
False or forced laugh Lachen mit yash-tsherkis
Family Mishpocheh
Family affairs Mishpocheh-zachen
Fan Focher, fochah
Fanny (buttocks) Inten, hinten, toches (taboo)
Farewell! Zei(t) gezunt!
Farmer Yishuvnik, poyer
Fart (taboo) Fortz (taboo)
(To) Fast-talk Shmeikel
Fat Shmaltz (grease or oil compounds)
Fat Fet (robust, plump)
Fated Bashert
(The) Fated one; the destined one Basherter
Father Tateh, tatteh, tatteleh, tatinka, tatteniu, foter
Father-in-law Shver
Fatigued Farmutshet
Feces (Dung) Drek (taboo)
Feeble-minded Tam chosser daieh; tamavateh
Feeding rabinnical students Essen teg
Feeling dizzy Shvindilt in di oygen
Fellow (young) who assumes airs Gantser mentsh
Female Nekaiveh (also means tart or whore)

Female Angel of Death Malech-hamovesteh
Female blabbermouth Yenteh
Female broker Meklerkeh
Female demon Klipeh
Female infant (affectionate term) Pisherkeh (taboo;
   Lit., Little urinator)
Female tricks Veiberisheh shtik
Festive Yontenfdik
Fever Kadoches, feeber, hitz
Fidgety Zitsen ahf shpilkes
Fiftieth Wedding Anniversary Goldeneh chasseneh
Fighter (usually for a cause) Kemfer
Filthy rich Ongeshtopt mit gelt
Finally Sof-kol-sof
(A) Find (bargain) Metsieh
Fine (upstanding) Balebatish
Finicky Aidel gepatshket; prietskeh (refers only to a girl)
Finished! A nechtiker tog!
First two words of mourner's prayer for the dead
   Yisgadal, vyiskadash
Five dolar bill Finef, finferl
Flattery Shmaltz (slang); drek (taboo)
(To) Flatulate Fortzen (taboo)
Flatulence Fortz (taboo)
Flavor Ta'am
(To) Fleece Yentz, opnaren
Floorshow Kabaret forshtelung
Folly Shmontses
Food forbidden under Jewish dietary laws Traif, traifeh
Food that meets rules of Jewish dietary laws Kosher
Fool Nar; slang—shlemiel, shmendrik, shmegegi,
   behaimeh, ferd, yold
Fool (self-made) Shmok (taboo)
Fooled Opgenart
Foolish Narish
(A) foolish, dumb person Shlump, shlub, zhlub

Foolish (fruitless) question Klotz kasheh
Foolishness Narishkeit
Fooey! Feh!
For a change! In a noveneh!
For better, for worse Tsum glik, tsum shlimazel
For nothing Umzist
For the sake of Vegen
Forbidden food Traif
Forbidden literature Traifeneh bicher, traifeneh literatur
Forget him! Ich hob im in bod!
Forget it! A nechtiker tog! (idiom) Fargess es! (Lit.)
Forgetful Katzisher kop, katz-in-kop
Forgive me Zeit (mir) moychel
(To) Fornicate Baren, trenen, yentzen (all taboo)
Fornicator (taboo) Yentzer
Fracture Broch
Fractured English Gebrochener english; gehakteh english
Fraud Shvindel
(A) free-loader Shlepper, shnorrer
Free-thinking Jew Apikoiress ,goy
Free-thinking Jewish girl Apikoiresteh, goyeh
Fried chicken skin or fat Gribbenes, grivvenes, greeven
Friend (male) Chaver (pl., chavairim)
       (fem.) Chaverteh
Friendly face Haimish ponim
Friendly term for anybody you like Bubbee (booh-bee)
Frig you! (taboo) Tren zich! (taboo)
Fringed garment Tsitseh-kanfes, talis koten
Fringed sleeveless shirt Leibtsudekel
Fringes attached to the four corners of the tallis (prayer shawl) Tsitsis, tzitz
From your mouth to God's ear! Fun dein moyl in Gots oyern!
Front row in the synagogue Mizrach-vant
Frozen Farfroyren
Fruit and nut coffee rolls Shnecken

Fruitless, endless matter Farshlepteh krenk
Full of care, anxiety Fardeiget
Funeral Levei-yah
(To) Futz around Patshken
(A) Fuss over nothing Machen a tsimmes

Gabby, talkative, shrewish woman   Yenteh, klipeh
Gadabout   Kochleffel
Gall (impudence)   Chutzpeh
Garden of eden, paradise   Ganaiden
Gargle solution   Haldz-shvenkechts
Gather pleasure   Shepen naches
Gentile   Goy
Gentile boy   Shaigetz (pl., shkotzim)
Gentile woman   Goyeh
Gentle   Gemitlich
Get a move on!   Gib zich a shockel! Gib zich a traisel!
   Eilt zich!
Get away from me!   Tshepeh zich op fun mir!
Get killed!   Ver derharget! Ver geharget!
Get lost! Go away!   Ver farblondjet! Trog zich op!
Get lost!   Gai kucken ahf dem yam (taboo; Lit., Go
   defecate in the ocean)
(To) Get rid of   Obtshepen zich
Getting senile   Aiver butel, veren oiver botel
Gimmick   Machareikeh
Girl of marriageable age   Kalleh moid
Gizzard   Pipek, pupik
Glass of tea   Glezel tai
Gloomy   Kalamutneh, kalemutneh
(To) Glow with pride and happiness   K'velen
(A) Gnawing, grinding person   Grizhidiker
Go away!   Gai avek!
Go away, get lost!   Ver farblondjet!
Go bang your head against the wall!   Gai klop zich kop
   in vant!
Go-between (male)   Mekler
        (fem.)   Meklerkeh
Go bother the bedbugs!   Gai bareh di vantsen!

Go break a leg!   Gai tsebrech a fus!

Go break your own head!   Shlog zich kop in vant!

Go drive yourself crazy!   Gai fardrai zich dein (aigenem) kop!

Go drive yourself crazy, then you'll know how I feel.   Fardrai zich dein kop, vest du mainen s'iz meiner!

Go fight City Hall!   Shlog zich mit Got arum! Gai shlog zich mit Got arum!

Go fight heaven!   Gai shlog zich mit Got!

Go flap your ears!   Ich hob dich!

Go frig yourself!   Gai tren zich (taboo)

Go jump in a lake!   Nem zich a vaneh!

Go mix yourself up, not me!   Gai fardrai zich dein aigenem kop!

Go peddle your fish elsewhere!   Gai feifen ahfen yam!

(To) Go somewhere unwillingly or unwantedly   Shlepen zich

Go split your guts!   Gai plats!

Go take a bath!   Nem zich a vaneh!

Go take a shit for yourself (taboo)   Kuck zich oys! (taboo)

Go to hell!   Gai in drerd arein! Ich hob dich in drerd! Gai kabenyah mattereh!

Go to the devil!   A ruach in dein taten's taten arein!

Goad   Utz

God   Oybershter; der Oybershter in himel; Got

God damn it!   A broch!

God forbid! (It shouldn't happen!)   Cholileh! Got zol ophiten! Nishtu gedacht! Chas v'cholileh Chas v'sholem! Umbeshrien! Umberufen!

God in Heaven, Master of the Universe!   Riboynoy-Shel Oylom! (Hebrew)

God in Heaven!   Got in himmel! (said in anguish, despair, fear or frustration); also, Oybershter in himmel!

God knows   Got vaist

God, our Father   Tateniu-Foter

God should hear you and favor you!   Fun eier moyl in

Gots oyeren!

God watches out for fools!　Got hit op di naronim

God will it!　Alivei! Halevai!

God will punish!　Got vet shtrofen!

God willing!　Mirtsishem (contraction of Im yirtseh Hashem)

Going into labor to give birth　Gaien tsu kind

Golden country　Goldeneh medineh (usually refers to the United States)

Gonorrhea　Tripper

Good-bye　Zei(t) gezunt. (A) Guten tog. Gai gezunterhait! A guten!

Good-day　(A) Guten tog

Good deed　Mitsveh

(A) Good-for-nothing　Groisser gornisht

Good for nothing!　Toig ahf kapores!

Good health!　Gezunt-heit!

Good health to you!　A gezunt ahf dein kop!

Good holiday!　Gut yontev!

Good Jew　Shainer Yid

Good luck!　Zol zein mit glick! Mazel tov!

Good luck to you!　A glick ahf dir!

Good Sabbath!　Gut Shabbes

Good taste　Ta'am

Good things (food, dollars, news, etc.)　Guts (gits)

Gooey food　Shmaltz, shmaltzik

(A) Goof　Shmoe (Americanism)

Goofy parents, goofy children　Meshugeneh gens, meshugeneh gribenes

(A) Gossip　Yachneh, yenteh; rechilesnutzeh; plyotkenitzeh

(To) Gossip　Shushken zich, bareden yenem

(A) Gourmand　Fresser

Gourmandizing　Fressing (Americanism)

Gourmet's delight　Meichel

Grace at meals　Bentshen; birchas hamozoin (Hebrew)

Grandchild   Ainikel; shtik naches (fig.)
Grandfather   Zaideh
Grondmother   Bobbeh
Grandmother's story (figuratively, a fairy tale, an unbelievable story)   Bobbeh meiseh, baba meiseh, bubbeh meiseh
Gratification (from children)   Naches
Grease (fat)   Shmaltz
Great!   Ei, gut!
(A) Great pleasure (usually food)   Mecheieh!
(A) Great pleasure (to meet you)   A fargenigen (tzu eich bagaigenen)
Great satisfaction   Mecheieh
Groan   Ech! (of disgust); oy, vai! (of distress)
Groans   Krechts
Groats   Kasheh
Growl   Burtshen
(To) Guard   Varfen an oyg
(A) Guilty person is always sensitive   Ahfen goniff brent dos hittel
Guy who desn't smell too good   Shtunk, shtinker

(A) Hag (also worthless) Shkapeh
Hanger-on Shlepper, nuchshlepper, tsutsheppenish
Happiness Naches, frailechkeit
Happy Frailech
Happy-go-lucky people A lebedikeh velt
Happy Sabbath! Gut shabbos!
Hard Shver
Hard circular roll with hole in the center like a doughnut Bagel, baigel
Hard doughnut with glazed surface Bagel, baigel
Hard-luck guy Shlimazel
Hard-luck sucker Shlimazel
Hard-working, efficient housewife Beryeh
(To) Haul Shlepen
(To) Have a yen for Farglist, farglust, glusten tsu, hoben chaishek tsu
(To) Have no end of brouble Hoben tsu zingen un tsu zogen
Have respect! Hob derech erets!
Have you finished the dirty work? Shoyn opgetrent? (taboo) (Lit., Have you finished fornicating?)
Having a ball! Laibt a tog! Leben a guten tog!
He aspires to higher places (beyond his reach) Er kricht in di hoyecheh fenster
He doesn't give a damn! Es ligt im nit in zinnen. Er hot es in drerd.
He doesn't know what he's looking at! Er kukt vi a hun in a B'nai Odom!
He eats like a horse. Er frest vi a ferd.
He eats as if just recovered from a sickness. Er est vi noch a krenk.
He has a cold. Er hot a farshtopteh nonyeh. Er iz farkilt.
He has odd ways. Er hot modneh drochim Er pravhet

120

meshugeneh shtik.

He has no say (authority).   Er hot nit kain daieh!

He has nothing!   Er hot kadoches!

He has nothing at all.   Er hot a makeh (boil)!

He hasn't got a worry!   Er hot nit kain zorg!

He makes a lot of trouble for me.   Er macht mir a shvartzeh chasseneh! Er tut mir on tsores.

He makes a mess.   Er farkocht a kasheh.

He-man   Mentsh, parshoin

He repeats himself; (he re-hashes things over and over again)   Er molt gemolen mel.

He ruins it.   Er macht a tel fun dem.

He should burn up!   A feier zol im trefen! Brenen zol er!

He should drop dead!   Paigeren zol er!

He should go to hell!   Er zol einemen a miesseh meshuneh! A gehenem oif ihm!

He should grow like an onion, with his head in the ground.   Er zol vaksen vi a tsibeleh, mit dem kop in drerd.

He should have lots of trouble!   A miesseh meshuneh! Alleh tzores oif zein kop!

He talks himself into a sickness!   Er redt zich ein a krenk!

He talks nonsense!   Er redt in der velt arein. Er bolbet narishkeiten.

He turns the world upside down!   Er kert iber di velt!

Head of a family   Balhabos, balebos, broitgeber, farzorger

Headache   Kop vaitik

Healthy as a horse   Gezunt vi a ferd

Hear ye!   Shema (Hebrew)

Heart ache   Harts vaitik

Heartbroken   Tsebrochen harts

Hearty laugh   Hartsik, shaineh gelechter

Heavy   Shver

Hebrew school for children   Talmud Torah

(The) Hell with him!   Kuck im on! (taboo)

Hello   Sholem aleichem, shalom!

Help!   G'vald!

Here, take it (in giving)   Na!
Here's to you! (toast)   L'chei-im!
He's a low down, good-for-nothing!   Er iz a niderrechtiker
   kerl!
He's a nothing!   Shmegeggi!
He's (it's) gone! Forget it!   A nechtiker tog!
He's hardly (barely) alive   Kam vos er lebt
He's restless!   Er zitst oyf shpilkes
He's slow as molasses!   Er kricht vi a vantz!
He's so happy!   Braiter vi lainger! Er iz azoy frailech!
He's thick   Er hot a farshtopten kop
He's thick-headed   Er hot a farshtopteh kop
He's worthless   Er toyg ahf kapores
Hifalutin   Feinshmeker
Hick   Yold
Highly connected person   Yachsen
Highly excitable person   Farshmei-iter, shvebeleh
   (Lit., a match)
(To) Hire   Dingen
Hodgepodge   Mishmash, kasheh
Hoi polloi   Mittelmeissiker
Hold on! (wait)   Vart! S'teitsh!
Hole   Loch
Hole in the head   Loch in kop
Holiday   Yontev, yontiff, yomtov
Holiday-ish   Yontefdik
Homeless wandering   Valgeren zich
Homosexual   Faigeleh (taboo)
Honor   Koved
Honorable   Balebatish
Horrible ending   Finsteren sof
Horrible year   Finster yor
Horse   Ferd
Host   Balabos (pl., balaibatim)
Hot bath   Haiseh vanneh
Hot-head   Kasnik, keisenik, hitsik

Hostess who serves you meagerly, gives you A lek un a shmek

Householder Balabos (pl., balaibatım); balebos

Housewife (efficient and comptent) Beryeh, balebosteh

How are things? Vi gaits? Vos hert zich?

How are things (with you)? Vi gait es (eich)?

How are you? (sing.) Vos machstu?

    (pl.) Vos macht ir?

How come? Viazoy? S'teitsh!

How do you do? Sholem alaichem! Vos macht ir?

How else? Vi den?

How goes it? Vi gaits? Vos hert zich?

How goes it with you? Vi gait es eich?

How is that? S'teitsh?

How is that possible! S'teitsh?

How much? Vifil?

How should I know? Freg mir becherim!

How's business? Vi gait dos gesheft?

How's tricks? Vi gaits? Vos hert zich?

(To) Humble somebody Derniderriken

Hurry up! Eilt zich! Mach shnel! Nu, shoyn? Yogt zich unter!

Hush! Quiet! Shat, shat!

Hymen K'nippel (taboo); b'sulim

I am disappointed.   Ich bin ahntoisht. Ich fil zich opgenart.

I'm dying for it!   Mein cheiyes gait oys noch dem!

I am fainting!   Es vert mir finster in di oygen. Ich gai chaleshen!

I am in a hurry.   Ich eil zich.

I'm not in a hurry.   Ich yog zich nit.

I'm sorry.   Es tut mir bahng.

I defecate on him (usually said about someone you're angry with, disgusted with, or rejected)   Ich kuck ahf im. (taboo)

I despise you!   Ich hob dich in bod! Ich feif oif dir!

I did wrong? So call me a "nut."   Ruf mich k'nak-nissel

I don't envy you   Ich bin dich nit mekaneh

I don't give a care!   A deigeh hob ich! S'art mich vi di vant!

I don't give a hang!   A deigeh hob ich!

I don't know.   Ich vais nit.

I dream of   Es cholemt zich mir

I hate him.   Ich hob im feint.

I have a choice?   A braireh hob ich?

I have a heartburn.   Iz brent mir ahfen hartz.

I have him in my buttocks! (usually said about someone you don't care for, or angry with)   Ich hob im in toches! (taboo)

I have no use for it.   Ich darf es ahf kapores.

I haven't the faintest idea!   Zol ich azoy vissen fun tsores! Ich zol azoy vissen fun baiz!

I have you in hell! Go to hell!   Ich hob dich in drerd!

I know.   Ich vais.

I like it. It pleases me.   Es gefelt mir.

I need it like a hole in my head   Ich darf es vi a loch in kop

I need it like a wart on my nose.   Ich darf es vi a lung un leber oif der noz.

I predicted it (my heart told me)   Dos hartz hot mir gezogt

I should have such a year!   Az a yor ahf mir!

I should have such good luck!   Az a glick ahf mir!

I should know from trouble (as little as I know about what you are asking me).   Ich zol azoy vissen fun tsores.

I should worry.   A deigeh hob ich.

I wish it could be said about me.   Ahf mir gezogt.

(An) Idea occurred to me.   Es iz mir eingefalen a plan.

Idiot   Shmegegi, vyzoso (both slang); idiyot

(To) Idle   Shlump (slang)

Idler   Laidik-gaier; batlen (if he's a perpetual scholar); pustunpasnik

Ignoramus   Am-ho'orets, amorets

Ignorant boor   Prostak, poyer

Ignorant Jew   Goy, shtik goy, grobber kop

Ignorant people   Prosteh mentshen

I'll give you nothing!   Ich vel dir geben kadoches!

I'm dying for it!   Mein cheies gait oys!

I'm not in a hurry   Ich yog zich nit. Ich eil zich nit.

I'm sorry   Es tut mir bahng. Es tut mir laid.

Impossible!   A nechtiker tog! Ummeglich!

Impudent fellow   Chutzpenik, ahzes ponim

Impure food (contrary to dietary laws)   Traif, nit kosher

In, into   Arein

In disgrace and humiliation   Tsu shand un tsu shpot

In good health   Gezunterhait

In-law   Mechuten

In-laws   Mechutonim

In spite of everything you do, it still comes out wrong   Aft tsi'lehaches, ahf tseloches

In the middle of   In miten drinen

In a pig's eye!   A nechtiker tog!

In the rear   Fun hinten; in hinten

In trouble   Ahf tsores

Incompetent person (who has perpetual bad luck) Shlimazel, loy yitslach

Inept person Shlemiel

Inexpensive Billik

Inferior Shlub, tandaitneh

Inferior merchandise or work. Drek (taboo); partatshnek

Innocent Got di neshomeh shuldik; nit shuldik

Insane Meshugeh ahf toyt; meshugeh tsum toyt

Insanity Meshugahas

Insignificant mistake Bubu

Insincere talk Falsheh raid. Drek (taboo)

Inspector or supervisor of Kashreth (Kashress) in restaurants or hotels who makes sure everything is kosher Mashgiach

Integrity Yoysher

Intercourse (sexual) Zetz, shtup (taboo)

(To) Irk Tshepen

Irreligious Jew Apikoires; shtik goy

Irrelegious Jewish boy. Shaigetz shkotz.

Irrelegious Jewish girl. Shikseh.

Is he bewildered! Er drait zich vi a fortz in rossel. (taboo)

Is he in a fog! Er drait zich vi a fortz in rossel. (taboo)

Is it? Tsi?

Is it my worry? A deigeh hob ich?

Is that how you talk to a father? Azoy ret men tsu a taten?

Is that so? Azoy zugstu? Takeh?

It appears to me Es veist zich mir oys

It could be! Es ken zein.

It doesn't make sense! Es iz nit geshtoigen un nit gefloigen.

It doesn't matter. S'macht nit oys.

It doesn't matter to me. Es macht mir nit oys.

It doesn't work! Es gait nit! Gaiet es nit! Se arbet nit!

It gives me a great pleasure! Es tut mir a groisseh hanoeh! Se git mir a groisseh ano-eh! (often said sarcastically)

It gives me pleasure   Es tut mir hanoeh. (often said sarcastically.) Es git mir a (groissen) fargenigen.

It hurts me.   Es tut mir vai.

It is conceivable   Es ken gemolt zein

It is imaginable   Es ken gemolt zein

It is (too) late.   Es iz (tsu) shpet.

It is not becoming   Es past nit.

It is revealed   Veist oys

It is said   Me zogt

It is very expensive (cheap).   Es is zaier teier (billik).

It isn't proper!   Es past nit!

It isn't running smoothly!   Es gait nit!

It looks like   Veist oys

It makes no difference (it doesn't matter).   Es mach nit oys.

It melts in your mouth!   Tsegait zich in moyl.

It never happened!   Es iz nit geshtoigen un nit gefloigen!

It pleases me.   Es gefelt mir.

It should be well!   Zol zein gut!

It should bang in your head (as it's annoying me)!   Zol dir alain klapen in kop!

It should happen to me (to you)!   Alevei! Ahf mir (dir) gezogt!

It should happen to me!   Mirtsishem bei mir! Ahf mir gezogt gevoren!

It should happen to my enemies!   Ahf maineh sonim gezogt!

It shouldn't come to pass!   Nit do gidacht! Umberufen! Unbeshrien!

It shouldn't happen!   Nishtu gedacht. Nit do gedacht!

It shouldn't happen to you!   Nit far eich gedacht! Loi alaichem (Hebrew)

It sorrows me.   Es tut mir bahng.

It stinks!   Es gait a raiech! Se hert zich a raiech Se shtinkt!

It will all work out. Es vet zich alts oyspressen.

It will heal in time for the wedding. Es vet zich oys-hailen biz der chasseneh.

It will suffice. Es vet kleken.

It will take a long, long time (till Doomsday!). A yor mit a mitvoch.

It won't help (any)! Es vet helfen vi a toiten bahnkes!

It won't hurt in making a match. Es vet nit shatten tzum shiddech.

It's a pity Nebach; a rachmones

It's a shame for the children! Es iz a shandeh far di kinder!

It's a steal! A metzieh fun a ganef!

It's bad manners! Es past zich vi a patch tzu gut shabbes!

It's delicious! Me ken zich baleken! Me ken leken di finger fun dem!

It's gone! S'iz oys!

It's gone; forget it! A nechtiker tog!

It's good for nothing! Es toig ahf kapores!

It's great! S'iz mir gut!

It's hardly worth the trouble. Folg mich a gahng (scoffing statement)

It's not to the point! Es past zich vi a patsh tsu gut shabbes!

It's not true whatsoever. Nisht geshtoigen, nisht gefloigen.

It's O.K. with me! Bei mir poilst du!

It's on his (her) mind. Es ligt im (ir) in zinnen.

It's over. S'iz oys.

It's perfect! Kosher v'yosher!

It's tough to make a living! Shver tzu machen a leben!

It's useless! Gai klop zich kop in vant!

It's worth nothing Toig ahf kapores.

It's your own fault. Me hot alain ungekocht.

(A) Jerk Shlub, shlump
Jester at a wedding Badchan
Jew who works on Sabbath Mechalel shabbes, shabbes
   goy
Jewish head Yiddisher kop
Jewish holiday Yontiff, yomtov, yontev
Jewish law (book) Talmud
Jewish native of Galicia Galitsianer
Jewish parochial school Yeshivah togshul
Jewish prayer shawl Tallis
Joke Vitz, chochmeh
Joy (from children) Naches
Joyous occasion (birth, bar mitzvah, engagement,
   marriage, etc.) Simcheh
Juice Zaft
Jumble Mishmash
Just great! Ei, gut!
Just made it! Kam derlebt
Justice Yoysher

Kasha with noodles Varnitshkes

Keep moving! Drai zich!

Keep quiet! Shveig!

Kiss my behind! Kush mich in toches! (taboo); kush in toches arein (taboo)

Knock on wood! No evil eye! (some say "Don't give me a canary.") Kain einhoreh (also, kain ain-einoreh).

Knot K'nippel

Know-it-all, who really doesn't know it all (sarcastic) Macht zich far a gantsen kenner; far a ya-tebbeh-dahm; K'nacher

Kosher condition Kashress

Ladies' room Vashtsimmer far froien
Land of Israel Eretz Yisroel
Large as a mountain Grois vi a barg
Last child in family Mizinikil
Lazy man Foiler, foilyak
Leader of the Jewish religious community Rav, rov
Learned man Lamden. Talmid chochem. Ben Toyreh;
  Reb (used as title)
(To) Lease Dingen
Leave me alone! Loz mir tzu ru! Tshepeh zich op fun
  mir!
Lecherous old man Alter kucker (taboo)
Less than nothing Kadoches
Let it be! Zol zein!
Let me be in peace! Loz mich tzu ru!
Let's conclude this! Toches ahfen tish.
Let's end it! A sof! A sof!
Let's go! Nu, shoyn!
Let's have some quiet! Zol zein shtil!
Liar Ligner
Life Chei (numerical value of two Hebrew letters, cheth
  and yood, read together as Chei). Chei also means 18.
Lighter taper Shammes
Likewise Dos zelbeh
Listen! Her nor!
Listen here! Hert zich ein!
Lithuanian Litvak
Littered Ongevorfen
Little Bisel
Little bird Faigeleh
Little boy Boitshick (Americanism)
Little bride Kallehniu
Little cakes dipped in honey Taiglech

Little girl (affectionate term)   Maideleh
Little infant (affectionate term)   Pisherkeh
Little nothing   Pitsvinik; klainer gornisht, banimenish
(A) Little of a fool   Narishehvateh. Shtik nar.
Little ones   Pitzelech
Little penis   Petseleh (used only to describe infant boy!)
Little prig   Klainer gornisht
Little squirt   Pisher
Livelihood   Parnosseh
(A) Lively person   Rirevdiker; nit kain farshloffener;
   lebediker
Lively Russian dance   Kazatskeh
(A) Lively world!   A lebedikeh velt!
Living by one's wits   Luftmentsh
(A) Living doll!   Yingeh tzahtzkeh (young one); lyalkeh;
   tzatzkehleh (a very pretty or capricious one); tzatzkeh
   (take your choice!)
Living high off the hog   Leben a chazershen tog
Loaded (drunk)   Farshnoshket; ongetrunken
Loads of luck!   Mazel tov!
Loafer   Laidik-gaier, pustunpasnik
Long coat worn by religious Jews   Kapoteh, kaftan
Long dist ance operator   Tsevishen-shtotisheh
   telefonistkeh
Long, lean girl   Langeh dronitzeh; hoieher drong
Long may you live!   Lang leben zolt ir!
Long winter underwear   Gatkes
Look at him!   Kuk im nor on!
Look here, look here!   Zeh nor, zeh nor!
Look out!   Hit zich!
Loquacious   Yatatata
Lost   Tsemisht (confused); farfalen (physical loss)
Lot of nonsense   Drek (shit; taboo)
Loudmouth   Pisk!
(To) Lounge around   Shlump; patterren tseit
Lousy   Nisht gut

Low-class people　Prosteh mentshen; prostaches
Luck　Glick
Luckless person　Shlimazel
Lump of sugar　Shtik tsuker

Madness Meshugahss

Magic-worker Kishef macher, kuntsen macher, **Bal Shem**
(Hebrew)

Make a living Machen a leben

Make a major issue out of a minor event Tsimmes

(To) Make a nothing out of you. Machen a tel fun dir.

(To) Make fun of Choyzik machen

Make it snappy! Mach es shnel!

Making a livelihood Hoben parnosseh, machen a leben
(Americanism)

Making an outcry Machen a g'vald

Malaria Kadoches

Male infant Pisher (taboo; Lit., a urinator); mentshal

Male person Mentsh; kaddishel (one who can say
mourning prayers for his parents)

Malingering sickness A farshlepteh krenk (a sickness or
matter that hangs on endlessly)

Man (derisive term) Shmok (taboo)

Man (with worth and dignity) Choshever mentsh

(A) Man built like an ox Bulvan

Man of distinguished lineage Yachsen

Man who assumes airs Bal ga'aveh; grois-halter

**Man who behaves meanly, miserly, ungallantly, or
vulgarly** Rosheh

Man who builds castles in the air; never achieves anything
Fantazyor; luftmentsh

Man who lives by his wits Luftmentsh

Man who threatens Yatebedam

A man with contacts Macher

Manana! Kum ich nit heint, ku mich morgen

Manly Gantser mentsh

Manure Drek (taboo)

(A) Mare (also worthless) Shkapeh

Marriage   Chasseneh
Marriage broker   Shadchen
Marriage ceremony   Chupeh
Married man   Baveibter
Master of ceremonies at weddings or banquets   Badchan
Master of the Universe   Riboynoy-shel-oylom
Match (marriage)   Shidech, der (shiduchim, pl.)
Matchmaker   Shadchan
May God help me!   Zol Got mir helfen!
May God prevent!   Zol Got op-hiten!
May he break a leg!   Zol er tsebrechen a fus!
May he rest in peace.   Olov hasholem.
May it be so!   Alivei! Halevei!
May it not happen to you!   Loi alaichem! (Hebrew);
   nebach
May it not happen to you!   Loi aleichem! (Hebrew)
May no evil befall us!   Kain einoreh! Kain ein horeh
May she rest in peace.   Oleho hasholem.
May we meet on happy occasions.   Mir zolen zich
   bagegenen ahf simches.
May you be inscribed for a good year.   L'shono tova
   tikosevu.
May you live long.   Lang leben zolt ir.
Maybe   Efsher, ken zein
Mean   Parshiveh
Mean, evil person   Paskudnyak, parch, rosheh
Meat dietary law   Flaishiks (Meat must not be eaten
   together with dairy (milichdik) foods).
Mechanic   Shlosser, machinist
Mechanical man (robot)   Goilem, golem
(To) Meddle (as a spectator)   Kibbitzen
Meddlesome spectator   Kibbitzer, muttelmessig
Meek person   Shnok, lemeshkeh, kunye lemel
Memorial service   Yiskor
Men's room   Vashtsimmer far menner
Mercy   Rachmones

Mere bagatelle! Bobkes! Bubkes!
Mere messenger Shlatten-shammes
Mere nothing Shihi-pihi
Merit Meileh
Merrymaker at a wedding Badchan
(A) Mess (slang) Kasheh, mishmash, hekdish
(To) Mess around Patshkeh, patshken
Messenger Shik-yingel; shlatten-shammes
(A) Middleman (also a person who is neither smart nor dumb) Mittelmissiker
Mildew Farfoylt
Milked! Opgeflickt! Arumgeflickt!
(To) Mind something Varfen an oyg; halten an oyg; bal moifess
Miracle-worker Balnes
Miser Karger
Miserable weather Finster un glitshik
Miserable person Shlak
(To be) Miserly Zhaleven, kamtsoness
Misery Tsores
Misfit Kalyekeh
Misfortune Umglick
(A) Misfortune! (wail) Az och un vai!
Mistake (insignificant) Bubu
Miss Maidel, freilein, chaverteh
Mistress of a household Balhabosteh, balebosteh
Mix-up (slang) Kasheh, mishmash; kuckamaimie
Mixed up Tsemisht, farmisht
Mixed up emotionally Farmisht
(A) Mixture Mishmash
(A) Moaner Krechtser (also means a blues singer)
Moans Krechtst (verb)
Money Gelt
Money (ready cash) Mezuma, mezumen
Money goes to money Gelt gait tzu gelt.
Money on the table! Ribi-fish, gelt ahfen tish!

Money thrown out Aroysgevorfen gelt
Money tied in a knot in corner of a handkerchief
  K'nippel
Money wasted Aroysgevorfen gelt
Moocher Shnorrer
Moron Szhlob
Morsel Shtikel
Mortally insane! Meshugeh ahf toyt!
Mother-in-law Shviger
Mother's pet (favorite) Tsatskeleh der mameh's
Mourner's prayer Kaddish
Mourning period Shiva, shiveh (seven days observed by
  family and friends of deceased)
Mouth (unflattering) Pisk (moyl: mouth)
Mouthpiece Pisk
Mouthwash Moil-shvenkechts
Move, already! Nu, shoyn! Gai shoyn!
Mr. Reb., chaver, bruder; freint (salutation)
Mr. Slowpoke Kam vos er kricht.
Mr. Upside Down! (person who does everything in reverse)
  Moisheh kapoyer
Mrs. Chaverteh, froy; madame (salutation)
Much ado about nothing Ahfen himmel a yarid
Muddled (slightly drunk) Far-shnoshket
Muddled work, picture or situation Ongepatshket,
  tsepatsket
(To) Mumble Preplen
Mush cereal Kasheh
My enemies should live so! Meineh sonim zolen azoy
  leben!
My heart told me Dos hartz hot mir gezogt
My money went down the drain. In drerd mein gelt!
  Dos gelt iz tserunen gevoren!

Naive Tam, tamavateh
Naive person Kunyehlemel, shmo (Americanism)
Narrowly achieved Kam derlebt
Nasty fellow Paskudnyak
Nausea Chaloshes
Navel. Pipek, pupik
Ne'er-do-well Trombenik, nebechel, nebbish, nebach, shlak
Neighbor (from the old country) Lantsman
Neither here nor there Nit ahin, nit aher
Neutral food (neither milchdik nor flaishdik) Parveh
Newlywed (male) Yungermantshik
News Yedies; neies
Nibble between meals Nash, nashen
Nibbler, especially between meals Nasher
Night is falling. Nacht falt tsu.
Nincompoop Shmendrik, kunyehlemel, shlok
No evil eye Kain einoreh (also, kain ain-einoreh)
No good Kockamaimie (slang); nit gut; nisht gut
No-gooder Trombenik
No-good person Nishgutnick, trombenik
Nobility Yichus
(A) Nobody (male) Pisher (taboo); a gornisht; a nishtikeit
    (female) Pisherkeh (taboo); a gornisht; a nishtikeit
    (a pitiable person) Nebbish, nebach, nebechel
    (a little person) Vantz (bedbug); a gornisht; a nishtikeit
Noise Tumel
Non-Jewish boy Shaigetz, shkotz (colloquial)
Non-Jewish girl Shikseh (colloquial)
Non-kosher Traif, traifeh
Nonsenses! A nechtiker tog! Drek (taboo)

Noodle dough   Farfel
Noodle or bread suet pudding (frequently cooked with raisins)   Kugel
Noodles   Lokshen
Noodle pudding   Kugel
Not a word of truth in it!   A nechtiker tog! Also, nit emes
Not good   Nisht gut; nit gut
Not in reality; supposedly   Kloymersht
Not making sense   Nit geshtoigen, nit gefloigen
Not necessary   Nisht naitik
Not really at all!   Chas v'cholileh!
Not so bad   Nishkosheh
Not so fast!   Chap nit!
Not today, not tomorrow!   Nit heint, nit morgen!
Not yet   Noch nisht
Nothing   Gornit, gornisht
Nothing (of small value)   Kreplech (slang); bobkes (slang); chei kuck (taboo)
(A) Nothing, a pitiful person   Nebechel, nebbish
Nothing came of it!   Es hot zich oysgelohzen a boydem!
Nothing of importance!   Eh!
Nothing of value   Shmek tabik (bit of snuff)
Nothing will help you!   Es vet dir gornit helfen!
Nouveau riche.... Oyfgekumener g'vir; olreitnik (Americanism)
Nuisance   Nudnik; tsutsheppenish
Nutty   Tsedrait

O.K. Zaier gut; oisgetsaichent
Obey me! Folg mich!
Obnoxious person Nudnik, paskudnik, paskudnyak
(To) Offer unsolicited advices as a spectator Kibbitz, kibbitzen
Oh! Ei! Ei!
Oh, God! Gottenyu!
Oh, what a scandal! Oi, a shkandal! Oy, a skandal
O.K.! Let it be so! Zol zein azoy!
Old acquaintance Alter bakahnter
Old-fashioned taste Mein bobbeh's ta'am
(An) Old bum An alter trombenik
(An) Old man An alter kucker (taboo)
Old maid Alteh moid
Old-style orthodox Hebrew teacher in a "cheder" (one-room-school) Melamed (pl., melamdim)
Old witch Alteh machashaifeh
Old wreck Alteh trombenik
Omelet Feinkochen, feinkuchen
On the level Emmis, emmes, be'emes
On the square Emmis, emmes, be'emes
Once in a blue moon! In a noveneh!
One who stirs up things Kochleffel
One who tends to confuse you Draikop
Onions should grow from your navel! Zol dir vaksen tzibbeles fun pupik!
Only God knows Nor Got vaist
Orderly person Balebos; okuratner mentsh
Ornament Tzatzkeh
Orthodox Hebrew teacher Melamed
(The) Other's Yenems
Other world Yeneh velt, oilom habbo (Hebrew)
Ouch! Oi, vai!

Outcast Oysvurf
Overdressed Oysgeputst, oisgeshtrobelt, oisgetzatzket
Overdressed woman Oisgetzatzket; aribergechapt di mohs
Over-praise (slang) Shmaltz, chanifeh
Overseer Mashgiach
Owner Balabos (pl., palibatim); balebos

Pain Vai! vaitik
Pain (exclamation) Oi!
(Real) Pain (ouch!) Oi, vai!
Pale as a sheet (wall)! Blaich vi di vant! Veis vi kalech!
Palsy-walsy Aderabeh-ve'aderabeh
Pancakes (jellied or with cheese) Blintzes (and they must be rolled)
Panhandler Shnorrer
Pansy (male) Faigeleh
Papa Tateh, tatteh, tatteleh, tatinka, tatinkeh, tatteniu
Paradise Ganaiden (Garden of Eden)
Parasite Shnorrer
Parents Tateh-mameh
Parvenu Oyfgekumener g'vir; olreitnik (Americanism)
(To) Pass wind Fortzen (taboo)
Pastry Varenikes (special type). Gebeks.
Patienece (that can edure sitting) Zitzflaish
(A) Patsy Shnook, shlumpf
Pauper Kabsten, kapsten
Pauper in seven edges (a very poor man) Kabtsen in ziben poless.
Peace Sholem
Peace be to you! Sholem alaichem!
Peanuts! (small things) Bobkes, bubkes (If you're curious, the word for nuts, also peanuts, is "nislech."
Peasant Poyer
Peddler Hoizirer; pedler (Americanism)
Pedigree Yichus
Pee pot Pishteppel
Peeved Ongeblozzen
Peevish (pouting) Ongeblozzen
Penis Potz, shmok, shlang, shvontz, vyzoso (all taboo)
Penis (derisive and derogatory term for a man) Shmok,

potz (taboo)
    Shmohawk (Anglicized variant for "shmok")
    Petseleh (affectionately applied to infant boy)
Perfect Kosher (slang)
Perish the thought! Cholileh!
Person from Lithuania Litvak
Person of loose morals Hultei
Person who butts into everything Kochleffel
Person who carries on work or sport in a slipshod, unbusiness-like, half-assed manner Patsher
Person who does not abide by Jewish law Traifener bain! Traifenik! Traifnyok! Shaigetz!
Person who will do anything to gain favor Toches-lecker (Lit., ass-licker; taboo)
Person with a sweet tooth Nasher
Person with fine taste Feinshmeker
Pervert Faigeleh (taboo)
Pest Tsutsheppenish, nudnik
Pesty nagger Nudnik, onshikenish, tsutsheppenish
Petulant Baroyges, umgeduldik, kochedik
Philanthropist Baltsedokeh, filantrop; nadven (Hebrew)
Philanthropy (spirit of) Tsedokeh
Phylacteries Tefillen, tfillen (worn by observant Jews on head and left arm each weekday morning while praying)
Piece Shtik
Piece of luck Glick, mazel
(A) Piece of shit Shtik drek (taboo)
Pig Chazzer
Piggish person Chazzer (slang)
Pig's feed Chazzerei; also, slang for food unfit to eat or merchandise unworthy to buy or own
Pins and needles Shpilkes
Pious Frum (frimer)
Pious person Tsaddik, opgehitehner, shoimer mitzves
Piss (taboo) Pishechtz
(To) Piss (taboo) Pishen

(A) Pitiable person Nebach, nebechel, nebbish
Pity Rachmones
(A) Plague Makeh, finsternish, magaifeh
(To) Plague Tshepen, tshepen zich tsu
(A) Plague on you! A magaifeh zol dich trefen! A choleryeh ahf dir!
Play Shtik, drameh, pyesseh
Played-out person, even if young; a person unwilling to participate Alter kucker; oisgeputtert mentsh
Playgirl Tsatskeh, tsatskeleh
Plaything Tsatskeh, tsatskeleh (female)
Pleasantly plump and pretty (woman) Zaftik
Please Zeit zich matriach; zeit azoy gut; bitteh; zeit moichell
Please; I beg you. Ich bet eich.
Please forgive me. Zeit (mir) moychel.
Please keep quiet! Sha! (gently said)
(A) Pleasure! A fargenigen!
Pleasure (from children) Naches
Plump (woman) Zaftik
Policeman (slang) Shammes (actually a synagogue sexton)
Pompous woman Rebitsin (Lit., the Rabbi's wife)
Poor box Pushkeh (In every traditional Jewish home odd coins are put in this, particularly on Friday afternoon, before the Sabbath begins)
Poorhouse Hekdish
Poor man Orehman
Porridge Kasheh
Portable table Ruktish
(The) Posterior Toches! also tokus, tokis, tuckus, hinten (taboo)
Pot to defecate in Kuckteppel (taboo)
Pouting Ongeblozzen
Poverty Oremkeit
Powerhouse! A yung mit bainer!

(To) Pray   Davenen
Prayer book daily in use   Sidder
Prayer of mourner   Kaddish
Prayer shawl   Tallis
Pregnant   Shvengert, trogedik
Pretend   Kloymersht
Pretends to be ignorant of fact   Macht zich nit visindik
Prettier ones they bury! (The girl is ugly!)   Sheners laigt men in drerd arein.
Pretty girl   Shaineh maidel; tshatshkeh (slang)
Pride (unreasonable and stubborn)   Shtoltz, ga'aveh
Prima donna   Prietskeh, pritseteh
Princess   Bas-malkeh, printsesn
Privileged character   Yachsen
Procrastinating! (Manana!)   Kum ich nit heint, kuim ich morgen!
Profane   Grob
Proper   Kosher (slang)
Property   Balebatishkeit
Proscription against wearing clothes that are mixed of wool and linen   Shatnes
Prostitute   Nafkeh, kurveh, nekaiveh, zoineh
Proverb   Shprichvort (pl., sprichverter); gleichvort, gleichvertel
Puffed up (peeved)   Ongeblozzen
Puffed up with haughty pride   Geshvollen, ongeblozzen, blozen fun zich
(To) Pull   Shlepen
Pun   Vortshpiel
Punch   Chmalyeh, klop, zetz, shmeiss, patsh, frask
(A) Punk   Paskudnyak
Push   Shtup (also used for sexual intercourse; taboo)
Put up or shut up!   Toches ahfen tish!

Question Frageh, sheileh
Quick, quickly Shnell
Quiet, don't get excited! Shat, shat! Hust!
Quiet! Stop talking! Shveig! Shush!
Quiet! Shut up! Sha! (shouted)
Quietly Shtilinkerhait
Quite a job! Folg mich a gahng!
Quite well Gants gut, nishkosheh
Quorum of ten worshippers for praying Minyan, minyen

Rabbi Rav, Rov, Rev
"Rabbi dear!" Rebiniu
Rabbi's wife Rebitsin
Rabid fan (also an ardent participant) Farbrenter; chosid
Racketeer Untervelt mentsh, gazlen (slang); ganef, goniff
Rag Shmatteh, tranteh
Raise cain Hulyen
(To) Rape Trenen (taboo)
Rare thing Naidlecheh zach; zeltenkeit
Rarity An ain un aintsikeh
Rascally know-it-all Kolboynik
Ravioli Kreplech
Ready cash Mezuma   ⟩
Real article; the real McCoy! Richtiker chaifetz
Real bargain! Billik vi borsht! (Lit., Cheap as beet soup)
Real buy! Billik vi borsht! (Cheap as beet soup)
Real fine, honorable man Mentsh
Really a bargain Tahkeh a metsieh, shoin ainmol a
  metsieh
Really crazy Meshugeh ahf toyt
Really? Is that so? Takeh? Azoy?
Rear Hinten
Rear parts Hinten
Recite prayers over lit candles Bentsh lecht;
  bentshen licht
Recite the afternoon prayers Davenen mincheh
Rectum Toches(taboo)
Relative through marriage (in laws) Mechuten
  (pl., mechutonim)
Relatives Mishpocheh, kroivim
Religious Frum (frimer)
Religious dietary law Kashress
Religious functionary who performs the circumcision

Mohel
Remember? Gedainkst?
(To) Rent Dingen
Respect Koved, derech erets
Respectable Jews Balebatisheh yiden
Responsible Balebatish, achrahyes, farantvortlech
Reverence Koved, derech eretz
Rich Reich
Rich man G'vir
(To) ridicule Choyzik machen
Right Richtik; kosher (slang)
Righteous person Tsaddik
(To) Rip Trenen
Ritual bath (part of the orthodox bride's wedding
  preparation) Mikveh
Ritual slaughterer of animals and fowl Shochet
Robber Gazlen, ganef
Robot Goilem
Rogue Yungatsh
Roisterer Tumler
Rotten (decayed) Farfoylt
Rotten person Paskudnik, paskudnyak
Rough Grob
Roughneck Shtarker, yungatsh; (sarcastically, voiler
  yung)
Round dumpling (usualy made of matzoh meal, served
  with soup) K'naidel (pl., k'naidlech)
**Row of pews at the eastern wall of the synagogue where
  the foremost members of the congregation sit** Mizrach
Rude Grob
Rude, coarse person Bulvan, grober yung
Rude young man Grober yung
(To) Ruin you Machen a tel fun dir
(To be) Ruined Verren a tel
Rush! Eilt zich!
Rustic Yishuvnik

Sabbath (twists of white) bread Challeh
Sacrifice of atonement Kaporeh
Sad sack! Shmulky!
Salmon (smoked) Lax, lox
(The) Same to you! Gam atem! (Hebrew)
(A) Sap Shnook
Satisfactory Nishkosheh
Savory Varnitshkes
Say a few words Zog a por verter
(A) Saying Gleichvertel
Scamp Yungatsh
Scatterbrain Draikop
Scholar Lamden, ben toyreh
School Shule
Scram! Trog zich up! Avek!
Scrambled eggs Feinkuchen
Scream K'vitsh
Screech K'vitsh
Screwy Tsedrait
Scroll or the Book of Esther Megillah
Second rater Shlumpf
Self-made fool Shmok (taboo because it also means penis)
Senile Aiver butel, oiver botel
Sensuous looking (girl) Zaftik
Sentimental Shmaltzy, sentimentahl
Serpent Shlang (also big penis taboo)
Serves him right! Gut oyf im! A shaineh, raineh, kaporeh!
Sexton of the synagogue Shamas, shammes
Sexual experience Zetz (taboo)
Sexual intercourse Shtup (taboo)
Sexually attractive girl Tzatzkeh, zaftik, zaftikeh moid
(To) Shake and dance with joy Hetskentzich, tzitern fun
  fraid

149

Shame and disgrace　Mies un mos; a shandeh un a charpeh

Sharp (referring to clothes)　Yontevdik

Sharp practices　Genaivisheh shtiklech

She doesn't stop talking　Zi farmacht nit dos moyl

She has all the virtues　Aleh meiles hot zi

She should rest in peace.　Oleho hasholom.

Shit　Drek (taboo)

(To) Shit　Kucken (taboo)

Shit-head　Kucker, shtik drek (both taboo)

Shitty　Farkackt, fekuckteh (taboo)

Shmohawk　Anglicized variant for shmok (penis)

Shoddy　Opgekrochen, shlak

Shoddy merchandise　Opgekrocheneh schoireh, shlak vareh

(To) Shout for help　Machen a g'vald

Shove　Shtup, shtuppen

(You should) Shove it up your rectum　Zolst es shtupin in toches arein! (taboo)

Shove (or stick) it up your rectum!　Shtup es in toches! (taboo)

(A) Show-off　K'nacker, grois-halter, barimer, shvitser

Shrew　Shlecht veib; klipeh, mirshaas

Shriek　Kvitsh

Shut up!　Sha! Shveig! Farmach dos moyl!

Shy　Shemevdik

Shy person　Nebbish, nebechel, shemevdiker

Sick　Krank

Sickness　Krenk, krank-heit, cholaas

Sickness that hangs on　Farshlepteh krenk

Silence!　Zol zein shtil!

Simple-minded　Tamavateh

Simple people　Prosteh leit, prosteh mentshen

Simpleton　Nebbish, shlemiel, shmendrik, tam

Sister-in-law　Shvegerin

Sit in mourning　Zitsen shiveh (Shiveh means seven—

the number of days in the mourning period)
Sit on pins and needles Zitsen ahf shpilkes.
Skilled worker Balmelocheh
Skin someone alive Reisen di hoit, shinden di hoit
Skinny Oysgedarcht
Skol Le'cha-yim, lechei-im, l'chei-im
Skull cap usually worn during prayers and worn at all times by extreme Orthodox Jews—also worn by Catholic prelates Yarmelkeh
Slam Chmalyeh
Slap (open hand) Patsh
    (back of the hand) Frassk
(To) Slap Geben a patsh
Slattern Yachneh
Sleeveless shirt (religious undershirt) Leibtzudekel, tallis koton, arbeh kanfess
Slightly drunk Farshnoshket
Slime Shmuts
Slipshop worker or player (sports) Patsher
Slob Zhlob
Sloppy Ongepatshket
Slow Pamelech, pavolyeh, gemitlech
Slowly Pamelech, pavolyeh, gemitlech
Slowpoke Kam vos er kricht
Slow-wittedness Goyisher kop; kunyehlemel
Slumhouse Churveh
Small pieces Shtiklech
Small pieces of baked dough Taiglech
Small pockets of dough filled with chopped meat (like ravioli) or cheese Kreplech
Smell Shmek; also plural for shmok, penis (taboo)
Smelled bad (used only in reference to food) Shtark gehert; ge'avert
(To) Smell bad Farshtunken, shtinken
Smoked salmon Lox (pronounced "lahks")
Snack (between meals) Nash

Snake Shlang, (also, big penis; taboo)
(The) Sneeze confirmed the truth. G'nossen tsum emess;
  Genossen oifn emmes!
Snored Gechropet
So? Well? Nu?
So, so! (evasive reply to So?) Nu, nu!
So I guessed wrong. Nisht getrofen!
So I made a mistake, so what? Host du bei mir an avleh!
So it goes. Azoy gait es.
So now? Ober yetzt? Ober itzt?
So soon? Azoy gich?
So you say! Vais ich vos!
So what! Host du bei mir an avleh!
Social background Yichus
Social climber Er kricht in di hoyecheh fenster.
Society Chevreh; farein
Soiled Shmutsik
(To) Soldier on the job Patshkeh
Someone else's Yenems
Something decorative (like a woman) Putskeh
Something delicious Mecheiehdik
Something unattainable Telerel fun himel
Son Ben (Hebrew); zun (Yiddish)
Son-in-law Aidim
Sorrel grass soup Shtshav, tshav
Sorrow Fardross
Soul Neshomeh
**Soul condemned to wander for a time in this world because
  of its sins** Dybbuk
Sour cream Smetteneh
Sour leaves soup Shtshav, tshav
(To be) Sparing Zhaleven
(To) Speak through your nose (unclear) Fonfen
(A) Speaker's fluff, an error Ponf
Special bit of acting Shpilen shtik, rolleh
Spinach soup Shtshav, botshvineh

Spinster   Alteh moid
Spirit   Neshomeh
Spirit of philanthropy   Tsedokeh
Spitefully   Ahf tsi lehaches; ahf tsuloches
Split your guts!   Plats!
Spoiled   Kalyeh
Sponger (beggar)   Shnorrer
    (a hanger-on)   Shlepper, onshikenish, tsutshepenish
(A) Squealer   Mosser
Squirt   Pisher (taboo)
Stacked (referring to a girl)   Zaftik
Stammerer   Ikevater, hikevater
Star of David   Mogen Dovid
Start!   Fang shoyn on!
Starved   Toit hungerik
Steam bath   Shvitz bod
(A) Stink   Ipish, geshtank
(To) Stink   Shtinken
(It) Stinks!   Se shtinkt!
Stinky   Farshtunken (adj.), farshtunkener (noun)
Stockbroker   Mekler
Stomach ache   Boych vaitik
Stop annoying me.   Drai mir nit kain kop!
   Kush mich in toches (taboo, Lit., Kiss my behind)
Stop bending my ear!   Hak mir nit in kop!
Stop talking!   Shveig!
Stop talking yourself into illness!   A lung un leber ahf
   der noz!
**Store that sells cheap, inferior merchandise, second-hand
   or cut-rate goods where bargaining over prices is
   important**   Shlak joint (Americanism)
(A) Strange death!   A miesseh meshuneh!
   (Fig., It shouldn't happen to a dog!)
Stranger   Fremder
Street urchin (street Arab)   Yungatsh; arumloifer
Strong   Kreftik, shtark

Strong as a horse   Shtark vi a ferd
Strong-arm character   Shtarker
Strong character   Shtarker charakter
Strongly built person   A yung mit bainer!
Stubborn   Eingeshpart; akshen
Student of rabbinical academy   Yeshivah bocher
Stuff and nonsense!   Vais ich vos!
Stuffed cabbage   Holishkes, holubtshes, holebshess
Stuffed chicken-neck skin   Gefilteh helsel
Stuffed derma   Kishkeh (looks like sausage)
Stuffed fish   Gefilteh fish (usually made of chopped fish, onions and seasoning, and cooked in salt water)
Stuffed potato cakes   Varnishkes, varnitshkes
Stuffed shirt   Ongeblozzener
Stuffed up   Farshtopt, ongeshtopt
Substance   Balebatishkeit, iker, mamoshes
Sucker   Shlumpf, shnook, yold
Suckered!   Opgeflickt!
Suddenly   In miten drinen; miten derinnen
(To) Suffer   Plagen zich, leiden
Suffix to denote diminutive or affection   El, eleh
Summer boarding house with cooking privileges   Kochalain
Super-sensitive   Aidel gepatshkit
Superb (in taste)   Mecheiehdik
(To) Sweat out a job   Plagen zich, mutshen zich
Sweaty   Shlumpy (Americanism), farshvitst
Sweet cake   Shtrudel
Sweet carrot compote   Tsimmes
Sweet soul   Ziseh neshomeh
Sweet talk   Shmaltz, ziseh raidelech
Sweet thing   Ziskeit
Sweetheart   Neshomeleh! Tei-yerinkeh! Hartseniu!
Sweetness   Ziskeit
Swill   Chazzerei
(To) Swindle   Shmeikel

Swindler Ganef, shvindler

Swollen up; puffed up (applied to person with haughty pride) Geshvollen

Synagogue Shul, bes medresh

T.O.T.   See Toches ahfen tish

Tact   Saichel, takt, manyeren

Tail   Shvontz (also refers to a man who behaves ungallantly or idiotically)

Tailor   Shneider

Take it!   Na!

Take it easy!   Chap nit! also, Me ken nit tantzen ahf tsvai chassenes mit ain mol!

(To) Take pains   Zich matriach zein

(To) Take trouble   Zich matriach zein

Tale bearer   Shalatten-shammes

(To) Talk (idly)   Shmoozen, shmuessen

Talk oneself into sickness   Zich einreden a krenk

Talk to the wall (to talk in vain or to talk and receive no answer)   Red tsu der vant

Talk your heart out   Me redt zich oys dos hartz

Talkative woman   Yenteh, klaperkeh

Talking for the sake of talking   Haken a tsheinik

Talking through the nose   Reden fonfevateh; fonfen

Talking yourself into illness!   Zich einreden a krenk; zich einreden a lung un lebber ahf der noz!

Tall story   Bobbeh meisseh; nit geshtoigen

Talmudic academy   Yeshiva

Taste   Ta'am

Tasty   Geshmak

Tea   Tai; glezel tai; glezeleh varems

Teacher   Melamed, lehrer

Teamaster   Balagoleh

(To) Tear   Trenen, reisen

Teats   Tsitskes (taboo); bristen

Teen-ager (female)   Maidel, maideleh
      (male)   Yingel; boytshik; boytshikel (Americanism)

(To) Tell a lie   Zogen a ligen

(A) Terrible thing   Gevaldikeh zach, shreklecheh zach
Testicles   Baitsim (taboo)
Thank God!   Danken Got! Got tsu danken!
Thank you!   A dank! A shainen dank!
Thanks for a small favor.   A gezunt in dein pupik.
Thanks for nothing.   A shainem dank in pupik.
That's all   Dos iz alts
That's enough!   Shoyn genug!
That's how it goes.   Azoy gait es.
That's how it is.   Azoy iz es.
That's how the cookie crumbles!   Azoy vert dos kichel
    tzekrochen!
That's it!   Dos iz es!
That's nothing.   Ez iz bloteh.
That's what you say!   Azoy zugstu! (sing.) Azoy zugt
    ir! (pl.)
That's worthless   Es iz bloteh. Es iz drek. (taboo)
The business (slang)   Shmeer
The devil with him!   Zol er gaien tsu alleh ruaches!
The faster the better   Vos gicher, alts besser
The good old days   Mehlech sobieskis yoren (Lit., the
    years of King Sobieski); In di alteh guteh tseiten
The hell with him!   A brand oif im! Kuck im on! (taboo)
The hell with it!   Ich hob es in drerd! Zol es brennen!
The marriage is off!   Oys shiddech!
The majority rules!   Az drei zogen meshugeh, darf der
    ferter zogen "Bim bom." Az dos velt zogt shikker, laigt
    men zich shlofen.
The nuisance is here already!   Er iz shoyn du, der nudnik!
The real article!   Richtiker chaifetz! Di enmeseh schoireh!
The real McCoy!   Richtiker chaifetz! Di emmeseh
    schoireh!
The sneeze confirmed the truth.   G'nossen oyfen emess.
The whole works (slang)   Shmeer, megillah
Then   Den
There's a buzzing in my head!   Es zhumit mir in kop!

There is not   Nito
There still is   Es iz noch do
They don't let you live.   Me lost nit leben.
They say   Me zogt
They talk and talk and say nothing.   Me redt, me redt un me shushkit zich.
Thief   Goniff, ganef
This pleases me.   Dos gefelt mir.
This too is a living! (This you call a living?)   Oych mir a leben!
This was a pleasure!   Dos is geven a mecheieh!
This will do.   Es vet kleken.
Thrown-out money   Aroysgevorfen gelt
Thumb   Grober finger
Tickle   Kitsel
Tightwad   Karger
Tiny   Pitsel, pitseleh
Tired   Farmatert
Tired out   Oysgematert, ongematert, farmatert
(To do all the) Talking   A braiteh daieh hoben
(To have no end of) Trouble   Hoben tsu zingen un tsu zogen (Lit., To have to sing and to talk)
To life!   Le'chayim! Lechei-yim!
To your health!   Le'chayim! Lechei-yim!
Toes   Fisfinger, shpitsfinger
Too bad!   Az och un vai!
Too bad (novel complaint) that the bride is too pretty   A chissoren di kaleh iz tsu shain
Too costly   Tsufil, tsu tei'er
Too dear   Tsufil, tsu tei'er
Too late   Noch ne-ileh! Tsu shpait!
Too much   Tsufil
Tough guy   Shtarker; k'nacker
Tough luck!   Az och un vai!
Toy (doo-dad)   Tshatshki, tsatskeh
Traditional higher school   Yeshiva

Tragedy   Umglick, tragedyeh
Travel in good health!   For gezunterhait!
Treasury of Jewish law, interpreting the Torah (five books of Moses) into livable law   Talmud
(A) Treat (food)   Meichel, nash
Tremendous purchase (bargain)   Metsieh
Tricks   Shtiklech, kuntzen
Trickster   Mamzer, draikop, opnarer
Tricky doings   Gehnaivisheh shtiklech
Trifles   Shmontses, bobkes, bubkes
Triflings   Shmontses, bobkes, bubkes
Trouble-maker   Er kricht oyf di gleicheh vent
Troubles   Tsores (sing., tsoreh)
Troublesome wife   Shlang (slang, also means penis—taboo); shlecht veib; shlok
Truth   Emmis, emmes
Tub   Vaneh

Ugly Mies

Ugly thing or person Mieskeit

Unattainable Telerel fun himmel

Unconscious Chaloshes

Uncouth person Grober, grober mentsh, grobyan, grubyan

Uncouth young man Grober yung

Underwear (long, winter) Gatkes

(An) Unfortunate Kalyekeh

Ungraceful person Klotz

Unhurried Gemitlich

Unkempt Shlumpy, shlumperdik

Unlucky one Shlimazel

(An) Unlucky person is a dead person A mentsh on glik iz a toyter mentsh

Unlucky, pitiable person Nebach, shlimazel, nebbishel, nebachel

Unmarried girl Maidel (young one); moid (older one); b'suleh (virgin)

Unmarried man Bocher

Unnecessary Nisht, naitek

Unpalatable food Chazzerei, men ken es in moil nit nemen

Unsteady Shvindeldik, shokeldik

Untidy person Shlump, shlumper

Untrustworthy person Mamzer, draikop

Unwanted (companion or) follower Noch-shlepper; tsutsheppenish; onshikenish

Uproar Tumel

Upstart Oyfgekumener

(To) Urinate Pishen

Urinator Pisher (taboo, derogatory term applied to adult; affectionately applied to infant)

Urine Pishechtz (taboo)

Utter misery Gehakteh tsores; gebrenteh tsores

Vagina Loch, peeric, pirgeh, k'nish (all taboo)
Very little A biseleh
(A) Very poor man Kabtzen in ziben poless
Very wealthy (slang) Ongeshtopt; ongeshtopt mit gelt
Vicious animal (usually refers to an inhuman person)
  Baizeh chei-eh
Virgin B'suleh
Virginity K'nippel, b'sulehshaft
Virtue Meileh
(To) Visit Kumen tsu gast; gaien tsu gast
Vulgar Prost; grobyungish
Vulgar man (one without manners) Balagoleh, prostak,
  proster mentsh
Vulgar people Prosteh leit, prosteh mentshen, prostaches

Wail of sorrow   G'vald!

Wait   Vart

Walk on toes   Gain oif di shpitsfinger

Wallop   Klop, shmeis, zetz, chmalyeh

(To) Wander (to be lost)   Blonjen

(To) Wander around aimlessly   Valgeren zich, voglen

Wandered around   Arumgevolgert; arumgevalgert

Washroom   Vashtsimmer

Watch out (to mind)   Varfen an oyg

Watch yourself as if a fire threatened!   Hit zich vi fun a
  feier!

Watchman   Shoymer, vechter

We shall say grace.   Mir vellen bentshen.

We try harder!   Mir bamien zich shtarker!

We'll bury him!   Mir velen im bagroben!

Weakling   Nebbish, nebachel, k'vatsh

Weakness   Chaloshes (faintness); shvachkeit

Wealth   Reich

(Very) Wealthy (slang)   Ongeshtopt (overly stuffed)

Wear it in good health!   Trog es gezunterhait!

Wee (very small)   Pitsel, pitseleh

Well?   Nu?

Well done! Well said!   A leben ahf dein kop!
  (complimentary)

Well said!   Zaier shain gezogt! Gut gezogt!

What a . . . !   Sara . . . !

**What a sober man has on his mind (lung), a drunkard has
  on his tongue.**   Vos bei a nichteren oyfen lung, iz bei
  a shikkeren oyfen tsung.

What are they lacking?   Vos felt zai?

What are you bothering me for?   Vos draist mir dem kop?

What are you saying?   Vos zogt ir?

What are you fooling around for?   Vos barist du?

What are you screwing around for? Vos barist du?
(taboo)

What are you talking about? Vos ret ir epes?

What are you talking my head off for? Vos hakst du mir
in kop?

What did I need it for? Tsu vos hob ich dos gedarft?

What difference does it make? Vos macht dos oys?
Vos iz der chil'lek?

What difference does it make as long as he makes a living?
Nifter-shmifter, a leben macht er? (Lit., "nifter" means
dead)

What difference does it make to me? Vos macht es mir
oys?

What do I care? Vos art es mich?

What do you hear around? Vos hert zich?

What does it lead to? Vos iz der tachlis?

What does it matter (to me)? Vos art es (mich)?
     (to you)? Vos art eich? S'art eich?

What does it mean? Vos maint es?

What else? Vo den? Vos noch?

What is the name of . . . ? Vi ruft men . . . ?
Vi haist es . . . ?

What is the trick? Vos iz di chochmeh?

What kind of a . . . ? Sara . . . ?

What matters it to you? S'art eich? Vos art es eich?

What then? Vo den? Vos noch?

What will be? (Que sera?) Vos vet zein

What's cooking? Vos tut zich? Vos kocht zich in teppel?

What's going on? Vos tut zich?

What's new? Vos hert zich epes neies?

What's on his mind is on his tongue Vos ahfen lung iz
ahfen tsung

What's the matter? Vos iz?

What's the outcome? Vos iz di untershteh shureh?

What's the point? Vos iz di untershteh shureh?

What's the purpose? Vos iz der tachlis?

What's the trick? Vos iz di chochmeh?
What's wrong with you? Vos iz mit dir? Vos felt dir?
What's your name? Vi haistu? Vi ruft men eich?
When I eat, they can all go to hell! Ven ich ess, hob ich zai alleh in drerd.
When people talk about something, it is probably true. Az es klingt, iz misstomeh chogeh.
Where are you going? Vuhin gaistu? Vu gaistu?
Where does it hurt you? Vu ut dir vai?
Where the devil says "good morning" Vu der ruach zogt "gut morgen"
Whine K'vetsh, klogen
(A) Whiner A k'vetsher, a k'vatsh, a k'vetsh
Whirring noise Zhumet, zhumerei
Whiskey Bronfen, shnapps, mashkeh
(A) Whisper Shushkeh
(To) Whisper Shushken zich
Who knows! Freg mir becherim! (slang); Ver vaist? (Lit.)
Who would have believed it? Ver volt dos geglaibt?
Whom are you fooling? Vemen baristu? Vemen narstu?
Whom are you kidding? Vemen baristu?
Whore Kurveh, nafkeh, nekaiveh
Whorehouse Bordel, shandhoiz, nafkeh bayis
Whoremaster Yentzer
Why should I do it? Folg mich a gang! (sarcastically)! Farvos zol ich es tun? (Lit.)
Wider than longer Braiter vi lainger
Wife of a chazen Chazenteh
Wife of a melamed Melamedkeh
Wife of a rabbi Rebitsin
Wig Shaitel, (sheitel)
Wild Jewish boy Shaigetz, tsevildeveter
Wild Jewish girl Shikseh, vildeh moid
(A) Wild man! A vilder mentsh!
(A) Wild one! A vilder mentsh!
(To) Win gin rummy game without opponent scoring

Shneider (Colloquial)
Wisdom Chochmeh
Wisecrack Gleichvertel
(A) Wise guy K'nacker, chochem, chochem attick
Wise man Chochem
(To) Wish lots of trouble on someone A miesseh meshuneh!
Witch Machashaifeh
Without means (poor) Orehman
Witticism Gleichvertel (also used sarcastically) chochmeh
Woe! Vai!
Woe be to it! Och un vai!
Woe is me! Oi! Vai is mir! A klug iz mir! A broch tsu mir!
Woman in labor Kimpetoren
Woman of great beauty Yefayfiyeh; shainkeit
Woman prayer leader Zogerkeh
(To) Work or play half-heartedly Patshkeh, patshken
(To) Work hard Plagen zich; mutshen zich; mordeven zich
Worked to death Oysgemutshet
(A) Worker who does a job insufficiently gives you A lek un a shmek
Working on Sabbath Mechalel Shabbes; shabbes goy.
World to come Yeneh velt; oilem habbo (Hebrew)
Worn out Oysgemahtert, farmutshet
Worried Fardeiget
Worthless Gornit vert; shkapeh, bobkes, tinif (all slang); chei kuck! (taboo)
Worthless clothing Shmatteh; tranteh
Would that it come true! Alevei! Halevai!
Wound Makeh, vund
Wretch Shlak, shlok
Wrong Kalyeh, shlecht

Yearly remembrance of the dead Yortzeit
You already forgot? Host shoyn fargessen?
You can burst? Me ken tsezetzt veren!
You can go crazy! Me ken meshugeh veren!
You can vomit from this! Me ken brechen fun dem!
You can't dance at two weddings simultaneously. Me ken nit tantzen ahf tsvai chassenes inainem.
You can't get rid of it. Me ken nit poter veren!
You don't frighten me! Gai shtrasheh di gens!
Mich shrekt men nit!
You don't have to be pretty if you have charm. Me darf nit zein shain; me darf hoben chain.
You don't show a fool something half-finished. A nar veist men nit kain halbeh arbet.
You fool, you! Nar ainer!
You ought to be ashamed of yourself! Shemen zolstu zich in dein veiten haldz!
You please me a great deal. Ir gefelt mir zaier.
You should choke on it! Dershtikt zolstu veren!
You should get a stomach cramp! Se zol dich chapen beim boych! Se zol dir grihmen in boych!
You should live (and be well)! A leben ahf dir
Zolst leben un zein gezunt!
You should live so! Zolstu azoy laiben!
You should swell up like a mountain! Zolst geshvollen veren vi a barg!
You shouldn't know from bad! Zolst nit vissen fun kain shlechts.
You understand? Farshtaist?
Young and old Kind un kait; yung un alt
Young doll Yingeh tsahtskeh; yefaiyfiyeh
(A) Young, vigorous lad Yungermantshik, chevrehman
Youngest child in family Mizinikil

You're all set! Zeit ir doch ahfen ferd!

You're not making sense. Nisht geshtoigen, nisht
  gefloigen.

You're welcome! Nito farvos!

You're welcome (in my home). Shmirt zich oys di shich.

Yummy-yummy! Se tsegait zich in moyl!

Jewish Interest Books Ordering Information

Thank you for buying this book!

Carol Publishing Group offers many books of Jewish Interest—from History to Current Events...from Dictionaries to studies of Jewish Holidays and Culture, and more.

Ask for any of the books listed below at your bookstore. Or to order direct from the publisher, call 1-800-447-BOOK (MasterCard or Visa), or send a check or money order for the books purchased (plus $3.00 shipping and handling for the first book ordered and 50 for each additional book) to Carol Publishing Group, 120 Enterprise Avenue, Dept. 347 Secaucus, NJ 07094.

A Complete Listing of Jewish Interest Books From Carol Publishing Group

The Bar/Bat Mitzvah Survival Guide by Randi Reisfeld; Paperback $9.95 (#51295)

Blood and Banquets: A Berlin Social Diary by Bella Fromm; introduction by Judith Rossner; Hardcover $21.95 (#72055)

Dictionary of Judaism: The Tenets, Rites, Customs and Concepts of Judaism, edited by Dagobert D. Runes; Paperback $8.95 (#50787)

A Dictionary of Yiddish Slang and Idioms by Fred A. Kogos; Paperback $7.95 (#50347)

Evenings With Horowitz: An Intimate Portrait by David Dubal; Hardcover $21.95 (#72094)

Gut Yuntif, Gut Yohr by Maria B. Jaffe; Paperback $7.95 (#50390)

Instant Yiddish by Fred A. Kogos; Paperback $5.95 (#51154)

Jewish Holidays and Festivals by Isidor Margolis & Sidney L. Markowitz; Paperback $5.95 (#50285)

The Jewish Image in American Film by Lester D. Friedman; Oversized paperback illustrated with photos throughout, $15.95 (#51219)

(Prices subject to change; books subject to availability)

Moni: A Novel of Auschwitz by Ka-Tzetnik 135633; Paperback $7.95 (#51022)

The New Israelis: An Intimate View of a Changing People by Yossi Melman; Hardcover $19.95 (#72129)

No Sanctuary: The True Story of a Rabbi's Deadly Affair by Michele Samit; Hardcover $19.95 (#72182)

1001 Yiddish Proverbs by Fred Kogos; Paperback $6.95 (#50455)

Out of My Later Years by Albert Einstein; Paperback $9.95 (#50357)

Out of the Shadows: A Photographic Portrait of Jewish Life in Central Europe Since the Holocaust by Edward Serotta; Hardcover illustrated with photos throughout $49.95 (#72088)

A Spy in Canaan: My Life as a Jewish American Businessman Who Spied For Israel in Arab Lands by Howard H. Schack; Hardcover $19.95 (#72178)

The Way of Man by Martin Buber; Paperback $4.95 (#50024)

The World As I See It by Albert Einstein; Paperback $7.95 (#50711)